THE BIBLE DIET

BY

RICHARD H. MAYS, M.D.

Bloomington, IN  Milton Keynes, UK

AuthorHouse™
1663 Liberty Drive, Suite 200
Bloomington, IN 47403
www.authorhouse.com
Phone: 1-800-839-8640

AuthorHouse™ UK Ltd.
500 Avebury Boulevard
Central Milton Keynes, MK9 2BE
www.authorhouse.co.uk
Phone: 08001974150

© *2006 Richard H. Mays, M.D.. All rights reserved.*

*No part of this book may be reproduced, stored in
a retrieval system, or transmitted by any means
without the written permission of the author.*

First published by AuthorHouse 3/7/2006
ISBN: 1-4208-6957-4 (sc)

Printed in the United States of America
Bloomington, Indiana

This book is printed on acid-free paper.

    This book is not intended to take the place of medical advise and treatment from your personal physician. Neither the publisher nor the author takes any responsibility for any possible consequences from any treatment, actions, or application of medicine, supplement, herb or preparation to any person reading or following the information in this book. Readers are advised to consult their own doctors or other qualified health professional regarding the treatment of their medical problems. If readers are taking prescription medications, they should consult with their physicians before taking themselves off any medication.
    All scripture quotations are from the New International Version of the Holy Bible unless otherwise designated.
    Scripture quotations marked KJV are from the King James Version of the Bible.

Dedication:

To my wife (Autumn) and daughters (Heather, Rachel and Sarah) who gave up time with their husband and father to write this book.

Acknowledgement

Special thanks to...

Valerie who planted the seed to write this book many years ago in the College and Career Sunday School class.

Many prayer warriors whose prayers made writing this book possible. You will never know how much I appreciate you.

My mother and father who instilled in me a love for God's word.

My daughter, Heather, for her editorial work and transcription skills.

HE SENT FORTH HIS WORD
AND HEALED THEM...

— PSALM 107:20

Table of Contents

Dedication: v

Acknowledgement vi

Introduction ix

Chapter One: The Abundant Life 1

Chapter Two: In the Beginning 11

Chapter Three: Phytonutrients: God's Medicine 15

Chapter Four: The Seed Bearing Plants 21

Chapter Five: Fruits and Vegetables 41

Chapter Six: ...all the fat is the Lord's 53

Chapter Seven: Is all meat clean? 65

Chapter Eight: God's Dietary Laws Concerning Meat 75

Chapter Nine: Obesitiy and Tips to Lose Weight 83

Chapter Ten: The Defeated Overweight Individual 93

Chapter Eleven: Fasting 99

Chapter Twelve: Choices 103

Appendix A: The ABC's of Salvation 107

Appendix B: Personal Testimony 111

Introduction

I have been a family physician for twenty years. During that time I have seen and treated nearly every common disease and illness. One observation that I have made through these years is that a person's choice of lifestyle dramatically determines that person's risk of developing disease. In recent years, through the study of God's Word (the Holy Bible) and the review of scientific literature, I believe I have discovered with amazing clarity the reasons for this observation.

I believe the Bible contains dietary information that, if followed religiously, would prevent up to eighty percent of the diseases I treat in my practice. These diseases include, but are not limited to: heart attacks, strokes, hypertension, obesity, diabetes mellitus, many types of high cholesterol and triglycerides, some lung diseases, intestinal problems, cancer, arthritis, and even skin diseases.

Why am I so confident of this statement? My belief is based on a combination of my faith and my medical training and experience. I believe in a universe where there is one supreme God that has all the power, knowledge, and wisdom. Furthermore, I believe that God is immutable, which means that his wisdom never changes because it is perfect, thus I call it eternal wisdom.

I also believe this same God created us fully human. We did not evolve from a common ancestor of apes or any other species. This God then gave us a personal blueprint for life, or owner's manual, if you will, called the Bible. In this Bible, God gave us all the information we need to live a long, healthy, fruitful life. The Bible includes commandments for spiritual growth and development as well as statutes or laws for physical growth and development.

Many of these laws or statutes are recorded in the Old Testament portion of the Bible. God gave this information to Adam, Noah, and Moses and it represented divine wisdom. Since divine wisdom never changes, the same information given to these patriarchs must still be true today. Many of these statutes are dietary and I believe with all my heart that if they are followed strictly, they could prevent many of the medical problems we face today.

From the standpoint of my medical training and experience, I intend to show you in this book where multiple studies have proven the benefits of following these dietary statutes. Furthermore, my experience has taught me the hazards and deleterious results of not following these rules as well as the marked improvement in health and sense of well-being when these rules are followed.

In addition, God's word also contains non-dietary laws and statutes that, if followed, would eliminate many harmful habits that are deleterious to our health. You may be asking yourself, why would the Bible contain detailed information concerning diet? Why would God care what we eat or if we choose an unhealthy lifestyle? Even if He did, would the information given to man over 5,000 years ago still be relevant today?

These questions are answered in much more detail in Chapter One, but let me interject one thought now. If you believe in a Creator God, as I do, then you understand that we are His children. Just as we, who are human, want the very best for our children, how much more would God, the perfect father, want the very best for His children? This would certainly include good health and longevity as well as happiness and prosperity.

Furthermore, I hope to convince you that it is a spiritual act of worship to honor God by keeping our bodies healthy. If it is God's will that His children have good health, it is also to be expected that a perfect God would provide a method through which we can achieve that goal. I believe He did, and that He recorded it for all generations to read and know in His inspired Word: the Holy Bible.

Although this information was given to man over a time period of 3,500 to 6,000 years ago, I believe God's plan is just as effective now as it was then. Today, this dietary information is being proven by modern science to prevent diseases. In this book we will examine biblical evidence that God does have a plan for mankind to maintain excellent health. We will then look at what those dietary laws are and how modern science is proving that no healthier diet exists.

This concept of a Bible diet is not new; other excellent books have been written on this subject. So why write another book? The main reason is to attempt to show that following the Bible diet is more than just a good idea—it is Divine Wisdom.

We can all think of many things that are good ideas, but that does not necessarily mean we do them. We know it is a good idea not to smoke, but many do. We know it is a good idea to wear seat belts, but many do not.

Knowing that a certain diet is a good idea seldom results in compliance. We need more motivation to change our lifestyle. It is much easier to convince a patient to take a medication than to change their lifestyle. But if I can convince you that God, the Creator, has revealed to us food that maintains health and prevents disease, and that it is our spiritual responsibility to follow that diet, perhaps that would provide the motivation necessary for compliance.

The other reason for writing this book is to show what modern science is proving concerning the Bible diet. Good, well-controlled studies are now showing that the dietary guidelines given by Moses more than 3,000 years ago have nearly miraculous properties to prevent disease. Where did Moses receive this knowledge, unless it was by divine wisdom given by God?

Some of the study descriptions and technical terminology may seem a little tedious and boring to some readers. For that reason I have kept the use of technical descriptions to a minimum and have defined most medical and scientific terms as they are introduced. This book is written primarily to the believer in a Creator God, but the information in it applies to everyone. Even if you do not believe in God, these dietary guidelines will work just as well for you. Our father God loves all His children and wants the best for them, even if they are rebellious. Matthew 5:45 says **"... He causes his sun to rise on the evil and the good, and sends rain on the righteous and the unrighteous."**

I ask you to read this book prayerfully with an open mind and heart, and receive the knowledge that God wants you to know, so that Hosea's prophecy may not come true for you: **"My people are destroyed for lack of knowledge," Hosea 4:6.**

Chapter One:
The Abundant Life

The leading cause of death in our country is atherosclerotic cardiovascular disease resulting in 53% of all deaths. The second leading cause of death is cancer. It is now known that 60% of all cancers are related to diet. Furthermore, six of the ten leading causes of death in this country are directly related to what we eat.

As a parent, I do not ever want to see my children get sick. Likewise, God, the perfect father, does not want to see any of His children get sick: **"Beloved, I wish above all things that thou mayest prosper and be in health, even as thy soul prospereth," III John 2.** Jesus himself said, **"I have come that you may have life and have it more abundantly," John 10:10.** God wants us to have an abundant life. It is important to God that His children have as full a life as possible, and this certainly includes staying healthy.

God even gives us a promise to keep us healthy if we make Him the Lord of our life. Notice that this promise is conditional on us doing our part. This is the usual methodology of God: He makes a promise that if we do our part, then He will do His part. This promise is found in **Exodus 15:26: "If you diligently heed the voice of the Lord your God and do what is right in His sight, give ear to His commandments and keep all His statutes, I will put none of the diseases on you which I have brought on the Egyptians for I am the Lord who heals you."**

This promise is further alluded to in **Exodus 23:25 and 26,** which states, **"Worship the Lord your God, and his blessing will be on your food and water. I will take away sickness from among you, and none will miscarry or be barren in your land. I will give you a full lifespan."** These promises were made to the Jewish nation right after Moses had led them out of Egyptian bondage. However, as we will discuss in a later chapter, these and other promises were actually made to all generations.

Thus, God's promise to keep us healthy and free of disease is conditional upon our diligently following God's will in our lives and by following all his commandments and statutes. We will see that many of God's statutes relate to healthy living, including what we should eat and what we should not eat. I have often been asked, "Why do Christians get sick?". I believe one of the answers lies in this conditional promise of God. If we do not yield to God's will in our lives or follow His commandments and His decrees, including His dietary laws, then we can expect disease to occur in our lives.

Is it reasonable to think that God expects us to maintain a healthful lifestyle to receive His promise of health? The answer is revealed in **1 Corinthians 6:19-20, "Do you not know your body is the temple of the Holy Spirit, who is in you, whom you have received from God? You are not your own, you were bought at a price. Therefore honor God with your body."** This is elaborated upon in **1 Corinthians 3:16-18: "Don't you know that you yourselves are God's temple and that God's spirit lives in you? If anyone destroys (defiles) God's temple God will destroy him, for God's temple is sacred, and you are that temple."**

Do you get the message? *"If anyone destroy's God's temple"* and in the King James translation, *"If anyone defiles God's temple"*, then God will destroy that person (perhaps by allowing disease to destroy him). In other words, if we abuse our own bodies (God's temple) by not following God's dietary plans or by any other type of unhealthy living, then God is no longer obligated to protect us from disease. His conditional promise is voided because we did not keep our part of the bargain.

This point was vividly driven home to me by the following vision. I was driving to a local hospital early one morning to make hospital rounds. It was still dark and this is frequently a time when I pray and listen to God. This particular morning was no exception when suddenly a very vivid picture of Jesus driving the money changers out of the temple flashed into my mind (Matthew 21:12-13). Nothing I had been thinking about was even remotely related to this particular passage of scripture, so of course my first reaction was, "Wow, where did that thought come from?". As I contemplated that image, God revealed to me that Jesus aggressively cleansed the temple of everything that defiled or degraded it. The money changers, by cheating their customers, had turned the "house of prayer into a den of thieves".

In the Old Testament times from the days of the construction of the tabernacle of Moses to Jesus's crucifixion and ascension and until the Holy Spirit descended on the disciples on the day of Pentecost, God's presence on earth was limited to the temple building and specifically to the Holy of Holies.

In Jesus's days He made it perfectly clear that the Temple—God's dwelling place on earth—was to be kept clean and holy. He was zealous in cleansing the Temple. He was aggressive, he was radical, in cleansing the temple. He didn't follow what the rest of society was doing. He didn't follow what the religious leaders were doing. He went against the mold and protected God's temple from the money changers who had turned **"the house of prayer into a den of thieves".**

Today, if you are a born again child of God, your body is the temple of God. God in the form of the Holy Spirit dwells within you. You are God's temple: **"Do you not know your body is the temple of the Holy Spirit, who is in you, whom you have received from God?" 1 Corinthians 6:19-20. "Do you not know that you yourselves are God's temple and that God's spirit lives in you?" 1 Corinthians 3:16-18.**

How awesome is that? We, as born again believers, are God's temple. We should be overwhelmed and humbled by that fact. We should consider it in everything that we do—spiritually and physically.

The church is very good at teaching the saints (born again believers) to remain pure spiritually, but has not, in general, done such a good job teaching us to remain pure physically.

Both are very important, because we cannot separate our spirits from our bodies. In this life they are bound together. Thus, we cannot separate our spiritual life from our physical life—try as we may. The apostle Paul alluded to this in his letter to the Corinthians when he said, **"The body is not meant for sexual immorality, but for the Lord, and the Lord for the body. Do you not know that your bodies are members of Christ himself? Shall I then take the members of Christ and unite them with a prostitute? Never!" 1 Corinthians 6:13b, 15.**

Therefore, our relationship to Christ, and thus to God the father, is dependent not only by what we do spiritually, but also by what we do physically with our bodies and to our bodies.

Jesus cleansed the temple to get rid of "thieves". How many thieves are in your life? What are you doing to your body that steals away your health? What do you consume every day that is stealing your very life from you? Do you smoke, do you use alcohol, do you eat to the point of gluttony, do you eat foods that you know are unhealthy? If you do these things, they are stealing your health and are thieves in God's temple that need to be purged. You need to aggressively chase them out of your life.

What if we keep our part of God's conditional promise recorded in **Exodus 15:26? What is God's plan to prevent disease from coming upon us? Again, I believe the answer is found in the scriptures and is recorded in Exodus 23:25 and 26: "So, you shall serve the Lord your God, and He will bless**

your bread and your water, and I will take sickness away from the midst of you, and none will miscarry or be barren in your land. I will give you a full life span".

I believe one of God's plans to bless us and remove disease from among us is through our food. Specifically through the food that God tells us to eat and by avoiding the food that God, in His Word, forbids us to eat. I firmly believe this is God's plan to keep us healthy. There are indications of this from Genesis to Revelation.

In the Garden of Eden, there were two trees, one named the "tree of life" and the other the "tree of knowledge of good and evil". Man was forbidden to eat the fruit from the tree of knowledge of good and evil, and if he ate the fruit of the tree of life he would live forever (thus there would be no disease or death). Unfortunately, Adam and Eve chose to eat the fruit from the tree of knowledge of good and evil, and so brought death into the world. To keep mankind from eating the fruit of the tree of life and thus living forever in sin, God sent a cherubim with a flaming sword to guard the way to the tree of life, presumably until the world-wide flood of Noah destroyed it.

However, the tree of life makes another appearance in the Bible. In Revelations 22:2, the tree of life stands on each side of the crystal river that runs down the middle of the great street of the new Jerusalem. The Bible tells us it will bear fruit every month and its leaves are for the healing of the nations. No longer will there be any curse (or disease or death), but the fruit and leaves of the tree of life will, in fact, promote health and healing.

As another example, consider the exodus of the children of Israel as Moses led them out of bondage in Egypt. Moses had a major problem. How was he to keep these people alive and healthy as he led them through the desert wilderness? God's solution was manna, a divinely prepared and delivered food that looked like coriander seeds and tasted like wafers made with honey (Exodus 16:31). Every morning (except the Sabbath), it settled on the ground like dew. It met all of the Israelites' nutritional needs and kept them healthy. In fact, Caleb, after eating manna for forty years while wandering through the wilderness, stated that at age 85 he was just as strong as he was at 40 and **"just as vigorous to go out to battle now as I was then," Joshua 14:11.** God keeps us healthy by urging us to put the right foods into our bodies.

Let's look at the story of Daniel and three of his friends described in Daniel 1:8-16. Daniel and his friends were captives in the land of Babylon who were chosen because of their health to be trained to be the king's servants. They were assigned a daily portion of the king's rich foods (probably high in meat protein) and wine. Daniel, however, **"resolved not to defile himself with the royal food and wine, and he asked the chief official for permission not to defile himself this way," Daniel 1:8.** Obviously, Daniel took God's dietary laws very seriously. Daniel went on to ask for a diet of "pulse", which was mostly vegetables with some fruit and water. He bargained with the chief official to let him and his friends partake of the vegetables and water diet for ten days, and then compare them to the other young men eating the king's diet.

After ten days, **"they looked healthier and better nourished than any of the young men who ate the royal food. So the guard took away their choice food and the wine they were to drink and gave them vegetables instead," Daniel 1:15-16.** God's plan works!

The tragedy of the situation here is that many of us do not know that God has established dietary guidelines for us to follow. I did not know until the students in the College and Career Sunday School class that I teach asked me a few years ago to do a series of lessons on what the Bible says about healthy living. I agreed to do so, thinking that I probably could find enough material to last three or four Sundays. But three to four months later, I was still teaching every week on what the Bible contains concerning this topic, and I was amazed and changed by the wealth of material I had discovered. Although the information has been recorded in God's word, and has been there for the reading for over 3,500 years, most of us remain ignorant of it. All we know is that we are not healthy: we are overweight; out of shape; chronically tired; frequently depressed; suffering from many diseases, including [1]hypertension, diabetes, headaches, and [2]irritable bowel syndrome; having heart attacks, strokes, and cancer; and we feel helpless to do anything about it. But in fact, we have control over our own health through God's promises and by the lifestyle and diet we choose.

We can choose God's way and be blessed with good health or we can do it our way and suffer the consequences. I urge you now to choose God's way and aggressively purge your temple of everything not pleasing to God. The rest of this book will look at God's plan and his rules so you can know how to choose God's way. There are some concepts I want you to keep in mind while reading this book.

The first concept I derived from a combination of a phrase I was taught in school, "You are what you eat" and from the scripture **Galatians 6:7, "... for whatsoever a man soweth, that shall he also reap".** From these two statements I invented the phrase, "You reap what you eat". If you eat good, nutritious foods you will stay strong and healthy. If you eat junk food, you will become weak and sickly.

The second concept is that the closer a food is to its natural state (the state in which it grows), the healthier it is. The closer a food is to its original state, the better it is for us to eat. The less a food has been altered or manipulated by man, the better. A good rule of thumb is this: if God made it, then it is good to eat. If man made it or altered it significantly, use extreme caution. Have you ever realized that everything you really need in a healthy diet—the fruits, vegetables, whole grains, meat, eggs and dairy products—are on the outside three walls of every grocery store? Everything in between is not essential. That is not to say there are not some good products in the middle aisles of your grocery, because there are: frozen and canned vegetables, and some cereals, herbs, and nuts, among others. However, most of the middle aisle products need to be viewed with suspicion.

The third concept is simply a reality check. Sometimes we think we have the answers but inevitably if our "wisdom" differs from what God's word teaches, we will discover that we are wrong: **"Professing to be wise they became fools," Romans 1:22.**

The fourth concept is that *"What you do not know can kill you",* from **Hosea 4:6, "My people are destroyed for lack of knowledge".**

The fifth and final concept is that whatever you do, do it for the glory of God. **"Whether therefore you eat or drink or whatsoever you do, do all to the glory of God," 1 Corinthians 10:31.**

Now, with these concepts in mind, let us look at God's dietary laws.

Endnotes

[1] *Hypertension* - sustained elevated blood pressure
[2] *Irritable bowel syndrome* intermittent abdominal pain, gas and fecal urgency associated with constipation or diarrhea also called "spastic colon"

Chapter Two:
In the Beginning

The biggest finding in recent years concerning diet for the prevention of disease is that we need to markedly increase the amount of fruit, vegetables and grains we consume.

When I was in elementary school I learned some basic rules that have stuck with me throughout my adult life. One of those rules was "you are what you eat". This old but very wise adage is just as true today as when it was first coined. This saying could even be loosely used as a paraphrase of what God told Adam concerning diet at the time of his creation.

Our diet is so important to God that He gives our first dietary law in the very first chapter of Genesis, just one verse removed from the creation of man. In **Genesis 1: 26-27,** God created man and man's spirit. In the next verse, God commissioned man to **"Be fruitful and multiply, fill the earth and subdue it".** In verses 29 and 30, God's first dietary law is recorded: **"I give you every seed bearing plant on the face of the whole**

earth and every tree that has fruit with seed in it. They will be yours for food. . . I give every green plant for food".

It seems clear to me that God was saying you must follow these dietary instructions in order to have the strength and health to fulfill your commission, or loosely paraphrased, you will only be as good as what you eat.

A few things need to be noted here. First, God originally planned for man to be a vegetarian. In fact, man was not given permission to eat meat until after the great flood, as recorded in Genesis 9:3. We will discuss this further in a later chapter. Secondly, there were originally no poisonous plants, as everything created to this point was "very good," (verse 31). After man's fall from grace through Adam's sin, death came into the world (Romans 5:12) and so did pain, toil, thorns, thistles, and apparently poisonous plants. Thus, today we cannot eat every green plant, for some of them are poisonous. However, the importance of a mostly vegetarian diet cannot be denied and has been scientifically proven.

Now, let us spend some time looking at each of the foods listed in verse 29 in more detail. The first foods listed were **"every seed-bearing plant"**. This first classification of plants is that in which the plant's seed is the primary food source rather than the plant itself. This encompasses a large number of plants, including all grains: corn, wheat, rye, barley, oats, rice, millet, and buckwheat, and all ancient grains such as kamut and spelt (ancient relatives of wheat), quinoa (pronounced keen-wah), the basic grain used by the Incas in South America, and amaranth, the basic grain used by the Aztecs, as well as modern day hybrids such as triticale (a cross between wheat and rye). This also includes grain variations, such as kasha (roasted, hulled buckwheat kernels), polenta (corn or maize flour), and bulgur (a processed form of cracked wheat), as well as all legumes: beans, peas, lentils, soybeans, cow peas, and peanuts. It also includes a number of miscellaneous foods, such as potatoes (a tuber is just a specialized seed), many herbs (anise, caraway, dill), and sunflowers. This classification also includes nut trees, since nuts are elaborate seeds.

The second food source listed is **"fruit with seed in it"**. This is the group of plants whose main food source is not the seed or the plant itself, but the fruit it produces. This encompasses all fruit trees, vines and bushes, but also many of what we commonly refer to as vegetables: tomatoes, peppers, eggplants, cucumbers, squash and okra, for example.

The third food group listed is **"every green plant"**. This encompasses all plants in which the seed and/or fruit is insignificant as a food source, and the plant itself is generally eaten. This group includes a multitude of foods, such as mustard, spinach, kale, collard greens, asparagus, broccoli, cauliflower, cabbage, lettuce, onions, leeks, garlic, beets, turnips, radishes, and many herbs.

This vegetarian diet was all mankind ate for approximately the first 2000 years after creation. During this time man's average life span was several hundred years, although this was probably due to a multitude of factors, not just diet.

What has modern science learned about this vegetarian diet? It has been shown to reduce the incidence of [1]diabetes, high cholesterol and [2]triglycerides, hypertension, atherosclerosis (hardening of the arteries), and many types of cancer. These foods (fruits, vegetables, and whole grains) have also been shown to stimulate and enhance your immune system's ability to fight infection and recognize and destroy cancer cells. They have also been associated with a lower incidence of many forms of arthritis and skin diseases.

In subsequent chapters we will look more at the proven benefits of each of the three food groups described in Genesis 1:29-30, but before we do, we need to look at the source of these plants' amazing health benefits. Plants contain many beneficial vitamins, minerals, trace elements and fiber. All of these are important and beneficial to maintaining proper health, but they may not be the most important source of a plant's health promoting abilities. This honor may go to a host of recently discovered chemicals found only in plants, called phytochemicals, or more recently termed phytonutrients.

Endnotes

[1] *diabetes* - persistant elevation in blood sugar due to insulin deficiency (Type 1) or insulin resistance (Type 2)
[2] *triglycerides* - a type of fat that circulates in the blood stream

Chapter Three:
Phytonutrients: God's Medicine

An apple contains over 1000 different phytonutrients that make its vitamins effective.

For years, scientists have observed that populations of people who eat diets rich in [1]antioxidants (Vitamins C and E, beta-carotene, selenium and others) found in fruits, vegetables and whole grains, have a lower incidence of heart attacks, strokes and certain cancers. However, when studies were performed using antioxidant vitamin and mineral supplements instead of forcing the participants to eat the fruits, vegetables and whole grains, there was no decrease in the incidence of heart attacks, strokes, and cancer.

This apparent discrepancy confused scientists for years until the discovery of plant chemicals that were not vitamins or minerals. Originally called phytochemicals, and more recently termed phytonutrients (the prefix phyto means plant, thus "plant nutrients"), these chemicals represent the secret source of plants' health benefits. There are approximately 4000 phytonutrients identified so far, but only about 150 have been studied extensively and named.

Those phytonutrients studied have been shown to lower blood pressure, reduce cholesterol, fight cancer cells, stimulate the immune system, prevent blood clotting and act as antioxidants, protecting us against toxins such as air pollution, smoke, and too much sunlight exposure.

I look at phytonutrients as medicine that God put in our food to keep us healthy and that are more effective and certainly safer and less expensive than medicines prescribed by physicians. Phytonutrients are not usually found in vitamin and mineral supplements. You can only obtain them by eating the foods that contain them.

Many of these phytonutrients are plant pigments. About 2000 pigments exist in the plants we eat, including the 1300 known carotenoids and 150 anthocyanidins. Anthocyanidins are also classified as flavonoids since they impart to a plant its particular flavor. Carotenoids produce the red, yellow, and orange hues found in various fruits and vegetables. Carotenoids are also found in broccoli and dark green leafy vegetables, but their color is covered by the green of chlorophyll. Anthocyanidins give plants red, blue, and purple hues.

Deeply colored fruits and vegetables have the most vitamins and minerals, and are rich in flavor, but most importantly may provide the most health benefits because of their phytonutrient content. The exception is whole grains: although their appearance is bland, they are loaded with phytonutrients, including lignans, saponins, and flavonoids. Lignans and saponins have anti-cancer properties, and saponins may also help lower cholesterol.

We have discovered that each color food contains unique phytonutrients different from foods of a different color. Thus, we find that God has simplified our choice of fruits and vegetables by color coding them for us. We can classify fruits and vegetables into seven different color groups, each containing its own unique phytonutrients. These seven groups are red, red/purple, orange, yellow, green, white, and yellow/green. Eating a variety of fruits and vegetables of different colors every day obviously gives you the best selection of health promoting phytonutrients.

Some phytonutrients act like [2]estrogen in the body and are thus called phytoestrogens. These plants can be used by women to prevent hot flashes, night sweats and other symptoms of estrogen withdrawal. For many women they are effective and certainly safer and more natural than taking estrogen supplements (many of which are actually derived from the urine of a pregnant mare). In fact, if a woman is already on a diet high in phytoestrogens before entering menopause, she may not experience any symptoms of estrogen withdrawal. Multiple plants in our diet contain phytoestrogens but foods with especially high content include whole grains, soybeans, asparagus, broccoli, carrots, celery, parsley, yams, flaxseed, and nuts.

Furthermore, some phytoestrogens have been shown to act as both estrogen and "anti-estrogen". Thus in a premenopausal woman these phytoestrogens protect against high estrogen levels, which increase the risk of breast cancer, uterine cancer, blood clots and weight gain, by acting as "anti-estrogen". However, after menopause, when estrogen levels are lower, these same plant nutrients act as estrogen, preventing the symptoms of estrogen withdrawal without the changes in breast and uterine tissue produced by animal estrogen.

Isn't God's wisdom amazing? Could today's popular high meat, low plant diet be contributing to the explosion in recent decades of breast cancer? Asian women have a much lower incidence of breast cancer than American women and have been shown to have at least 20% lower estrogen levels, presumably because their diet is much higher in fruits, vegetables and whole grains and much lower in meat.

Some phytonutrients have been shown to reduce blood clotting and a higher plant diet may have the same benefit of taking an aspirin a day. Other phytonutrients have been shown to help repair [3]DNA and trigger the formation of detoxification enzymes in the liver. The best part of the phytonutrient discovery is that most of the 4000 plus chemicals discovered have not been studied, so no one knows what amazing health promoting properties they may harbor.

Now that we have discovered God's "medicine" that He gave us in our designed food supply, let's look specifically at some of the proven health benefits in the food groups listed in Genesis 1.

Endnotes

[1] *antioxidants* - blocks or prevents the harmful process called oxidation that causes cell damage, aging and many diseases.

2. ***estrogen*** - commonly thought of as the "female hormone" although it is present in men as well
3. ***DNA*** - the molecular blueprint present on chromosomes in the nuclei of cells. DNA carries the genetic information

Chapter Four:
The Seed Bearing Plants

Three servings of whole grains a day lowers the risk of heart attack by 33%. Each additional serving lowers your risk of heart disease another 10%.

WHOLE GRAINS

The first food source listed in **Genesis 1:29** is **"every seed-bearing plant"**. These are the plants whose major source of nutrition is in their seeds. This certainly includes all the grains. When I refer to grains in this book, I am always referring to whole grains, not refined grains. God intended for grains to be eaten in the same wholesome form in which they grow.

The closer a food is to the state in which it grows, the healthier it is.

The wheat grain (from which we obtain flour), for instance, is composed of three major components: The embryo, or germ (from which a new plant arises if the grain is planted; the starchy endosperm (which serves as food for the germinating seed); and the bran, which consists of several outer layers protecting the grain. Average wheat grain composition is approximately 2% germ, 85% endosperm, and 13% bran.

Refined wheat has had all of the wheat germ and bran removed. The wheat germ contains most of the nutritional value of wheat and the bran contains all of the fiber. After removing the wheat germ and bran, only a whitish-yellow, almost nutritionally void product (called refined flour) remains. Ironically, the wheat germ and bran are then sold in health food stores as "nutritional supplements" at high prices. Furthermore, the resultant refined flour product is, in many cases, bleached, to make the flour pure white.

This milling (the removing of the germ and bran) and bleaching removes twenty-six different nutrients, plus the fiber, from the grain that God intended for us to eat. Four of the removed nutrients (in a chemical form) are then added back to the flour, and the product is called "enriched" flour—although this "enrichment" process results in a total loss of twenty-two nutrients and all of the fiber from the original grain.

"Why spend money on what is not bread, and your labor on what does not satisfy? Listen, listen to me, and eat what is good, and your soul will delight in the richest of fare."
- Isaiah 55:2

I have not said much about fiber so far. There are two types of dietary fiber: soluble and insoluble. In general, fiber is found only in plants and resists digestion in human intestines. Soluble fiber is partially digested and thus has little effect on fecal bulk and bowel regularity. Soluble fiber delays the emptying of the stomach, which produces a full feeling (satiety). Soluble fiber also slows the absorption of digestible carbohydrates, which reduces insulin levels. The benefit of this is explained later in this chapter. Soluble fiber also lowers cholesterol. There are three types of pure soluble fiber: gums, pectin, and mucilage. A fourth type of fiber, hemicellulose, is both soluble and insoluble.

Insoluble fiber is not digested and thus increases fecal bulk and promotes bowel regularity. Insoluble fiber also increases the water content of feces, which speeds the transit time of stool through the colon. There are two types of pure insoluble dietary fiber: lignin and cellulose. Both soluble and insoluble fiber can bind undesirable chemicals and toxins in your food and remove them from your body.

In contrast to refined wheat, whole wheat contains protein, carbohydrates, fiber, calcium, phosphorus, iron, potassium, magnesium, zinc, copper, selenium, folate, phytic acid, a variety of fatty acids, and vitamins B1, B2, B3, B6, C, and E.

A reasonable question you may be asking yourself at this point is "Why?". Why is our flour refined if the process depletes the product of its most essential nutrients? The answer is not so readily apparent. It seems to be a combination of factors. The commercial milling of flour began about 100 years ago. Part of the original reason for refining flour may have well been "because they could"; because the technology existed with which to perform the process.

"Professing to be wise they became fools"
-Romans 1:22

Another reason was the mass production of bread. Refined flour makes a larger, lighter, fluffier bread than whole grain. Bakeries like the white color of refined flour. Their products were considered more attractive than their whole grain counterparts. Maybe a less appealing reason for refined flour was flour weevils. Many years ago, flour was kept in flour bins with sifters in Hoosier kitchen cabinets, and a common problem were little insects called weevils that contaminated the flour. The weevils were almost impossible to see in whole wheat flour, but stood out against the white background of the refined flour.

Refined flour and refined sugar are the culprits that have given carbohydrates their bad name. There are two basic types of carbohydrates: simple and complex.

Simple carbohydrates are chemically referred to as monosaccharides or disaccharides. Monosaccharides include glucose (the sugar our bodies use for fuel), fructose (fruit sugar), and galactose. Disaccharides include sucrose (table sugar), maltose and lactose (milk sugar). Simple carbohydrates include honey and molasses. Table sugar (sucrose) is derived from cane sugar, or beet sugar.

Complex carbohydrates are also called polysaccharides and consist of simple sugars attached together. They include the starches and fiber found in plants. In fact, almost all carbohydrates come from plants. The only major non-plant carbohydrate is lactose, from milk. Not all carbohydrates are bad. Carbohydrates are nutritious and beneficial to our health. In fact, they are essential to our well-being. They provide energy to fuel our metabolic processes and are components of cell membranes, nucleic acids (like DNA and RNA), and special proteins called glycoproteins.

Which carbohydrates are bad and which are good? (This is my opinion and not based on medical fact—yet). Going with the concept that the closer a food is to the natural state in which it grows, the healthier it is for us; I believe the carbohydrates that are tampered with by man are the ones that are bad for us. So, products such as refined flour, high fructose corn syrup, and sucrose, are the products that are causing many of our health problems, including obesity and [2]hyperlipidemia.

A carbonated soda pop contains 8-9 teaspoons of sugar.

For the purpose of simplicity (although not medically or biochemically correct), from now on in this book when I refer to simple carbohydrates, I am referring to refined flour, sucrose (table sugar), and high fructose corn syrup, which I believe are the main carbohydrates we need to eliminate from our diet.

Fructose (fruit sugar), although technically a simple sugar, exists in nature in the same form it is eaten and is better for us than sucrose. When you eat fruit, there is one extra step that your body takes to convert fructose to glucose, and this delays the rise in blood glucose, which lessens the rise in insulin levels. The lower insulin level is beneficial because high insulin levels promote weight gain and atherosclerosis. Even honey, I believe, is healthier than table sugar because you eat it in the same form it is found in nature.

The characteristics of the two types of carbohydrates stand out in sharp contrast to each other. Complex carbohydrates are loaded with vitamins, nutrients, minerals, and fiber. They do NOT promote weight gain. They lower insulin resistance and are digested slowly, resulting in a slow steady energy supply.

Refined flour and sugar products are almost completely nutritionally void, they DO promote weight gain, and they release their energy all at once, resulting in a sudden surge of blood sugar (glucose), and subsequently a surge in blood insulin levels. High insulin levels promote weight gain and accelerate atherosclerosis (hardening of the arteries), as well as cause many other detrimental effects on our health.

Thus we can see that the less grains are changed from their original form, the healthier they are for us. It is essential, therefore, that we eat only whole grains. This includes your bread, but also pastas, crackers, cereals (both cold and hot), pancakes and/or waffles, brown rice and soups containing grains like barley.

Read food product labels carefully. The label must state "Made with 100% whole grain", whether that be wheat, rye, barley, etc. Do not be deceived by phrases such as multigrain, autumn grain, and so forth. These products may look like they contain whole grain, but if the label does not specify "Made with 100% whole grain", they are not.

HEALTH BENEFITS OF WHOLE GRAINS

It is very clear from God's Word that grains in their natural, wholesome form are designed for us to eat. But is there scientific evidence that whole grains are beneficial to our health?

The answer is, of course, yes, there are several studies looking at the benefits of whole grains. We will look at the results of some of those studies and then we will investigate why whole grains are so healthy.

One of the largest studies to date on this issue is the Nurses Health Study, a prospective epidemiological study of more than 120,000 female nurses conducted by researchers at Harvard Medical School. In this study, researchers showed that whole grain products (specifically, whole grain breakfast cereals, brown rice, oatmeal, and bran) lowered heart disease risk in women to an extent that could not be explained by the fiber content alone.

Women who ate just 2.5 servings per day were at a 30% lower risk of coronary heart disease. A serving is defined as one slice of bread, one ounce of dry cereal or 1/4 cup of cooked cereal, rice, or pasta. This is an amazing reduction in the incidence of coronary disease, about the same as that seen in people taking the statin cholesterol lowering drugs.

Unfortunately, the average American eats only one serving of the health promoting whole grains per day, but an average of 5.8 servings of refined grain products each day, which does little except cause weight gain. (These statistics are from the USDA Continuing Survey of Food Intake by Individuals.)

A follow-up study by Harvard followed the eating habits of 75,000 middle-aged women for ten years. This study revealed that those who ate three servings of whole grain per day (including whole grain bread, cereal, popcorn, oatmeal, wheat germ, brown rice, kasha, or bulgur) were approximately 33% less likely to suffer a heart attack. Moreover, each additional daily serving of whole grains cut the risk of heart disease by another 10%.

Exactly how whole grains lower the risk of heart disease (the number one killer in the United States today) remains to be fully explained, but several factors probably play a role.

One of the reasons is the fiber in whole grain. The fiber prominent in whole grains has been shown to lower triglycerides (one of the fats in your blood stream), lower LDL (the bad type of cholesterol), lower blood pressure, improve blood glucose (sugar), lower insulin resistance (a major cause of heart disease), and prevent overeating, which of course reduces obesity. The fiber in whole grains also appears more beneficial than fruit and vegetable fiber in the prevention of heart disease. An increase of five grams per day of cereal fiber resulted in a 37% reduction in heart disease risk, whereas fruit and vegetable fiber had little effect on heart disease risk.

Another possible way whole grains decrease coronary artery disease is by being an excellent source of vitamin B6 and folic acid. Both of these vitamins are required to maintain normal levels of homocysteine. Homocysteine is an amino acid (building block of proteins) that has recently been discovered to accelerate atherosclerosis, the hardening of the arteries that promotes heart disease, when present at high levels.

Many grains also contain tocopherols. These are vitamin E-like compounds that serve as antioxidants. Oxidation is a process that occurs as a result of damage from oxygen (O2) free radicals. We are well aware of O2 free radical damage outside of our body. This oxidative process is what causes your car finish to dull and tarnish with age. Inside your body, this oxidative process damages the lining of your blood vessels, which causes an inflammatory process to develop. This inflammation is believed to be the first step in the development of the plaque which causes obstruction of the arteries, eventually resulting in heart attacks and strokes.

Of course, whole grains are loaded with phytonutrients that may be as important, if not more important, than fiber and vitamins in preventing heart disease. These phytonutrients include oligosaccharides, which increase short chain fatty acids in the intestines and lower cholesterol, as well as reduce insulin resistance. Flavonoids are antioxidant compounds that fight free radical damage, and saponins bind with cholesterol and wash them out of your body.

The evidence showing that whole grains reduce the risk of heart disease is indisputable. Likewise, there are similar benefits in the prevention of diabetes and reduction in the complication of diabetes in individuals consuming whole grain products. Again, the Harvard Nurses Health Study found that those individuals who consumed more than five grams a day of whole grain fiber had approximately 30% less risk of developing type 2 diabetes, compared to those with less that 2.5 grams per day.

Another recent study of men and women over a seven year time period found an indirect correlation between whole grains consumption and fasting insulin levels. The more whole grains eaten, the lower the fasting insulin levels. High insulin levels due to insulin resistance is the major cause of type 2 diabetes. High insulin levels promote weight gain; and obesity, of course, plays a major role in the development of diabetes. Diabetes is an epidemic in the United States today, so reducing the risk of diabetes is an extremely important role of whole grain consumption.

In addition to the benefits described above, whole grains are good sources of magnesium and vitamin E, which play roles in insulin metabolism. Moreover, the soluble fibers and indigestible carbohydrates found in whole grains are fermented in the intestinal tract by normal bacterial flora, and produce compounds that reduce insulin resistance.

Again, it is ironic that one of the most popular new types of medicines in the treatment of type 2 diabetes is a group called TZD's, which lower insulin resistance. It is such a shame, then, that a full 40% of Americans eat zero servings of whole grains per day—the food that God designed to lower insulin resistance.

There is also mounting evidence of the reduction in cancer risk by regular whole grain consumption. More than forty studies have suggested that regular consumption of whole grains reduces risk of twenty different types of cancer. The risk of cancer of the stomach, colon, gallbladder, liver, pancreas, ovaries, breast, and prostate can be lowered by 6-10% through regular consumption of whole grains.

This benefit may be partially due to the fiber content but also by the phytonutrients in whole grains, like lignans, phytic acid, and protease inhibitors. Lignans are estrogen-like compounds that seem to have anti-estrogen effects in preventing the harmful effects of excess estrogen, such as breast cancer. Phytic acid and other phytates slow the digestion of starches and help prevent oxidative damage to intestinal cells (thus reducing the incidence of intestinal cancer). Protease inhibitors help prevent the initiation of cancer in cells and inhibit the growth of already existing tumors.

Unfortunately, only 5% of all grain products eaten by Americans are whole grain.

"You reap what you eat."

You can increase whole grain intake by eating more oatmeal, bran flakes, 100% whole grain bread, low fat popcorn (unbuttered), baked tortilla chips, brown rice instead of white, whole wheat pasta, and wheat germ. A tablespoon of wheat germ blended into a cup of yogurt is a quick nutritious snack.

You can also increase whole grain intake by introducing some of these newer, less traditional products: amaranth, kasha (pulverized buckwheat), quinoa, spelt (a distant cousin of wheat), teff (an Ethiopian staple, it is the world's smallest grain), and triticale (a cross between wheat and rye). These products can all be purchased at health food stores.

LEGUMES

The seed-bearing plants also include the legumes. The legume family includes beans, cowpeas, lentils, lima beans, peanuts, peas, and soybeans. Peanuts are not nuts; they grow underground in a pod and are a legume. There are also dozens of varieties of dried beans, including pinto, white, kidney, calico, black, garbanzo, etc. Beans are complex carbohydrates loaded with protein, fiber, vitamins, and minerals, with very little fat. Legumes are also a good source of folate.

Legumes are loaded with fiber. Fiber is often classified as soluble or insoluble, and our bodies need both to stay healthy. Insoluble fiber has been shown to reduce the risk of colon cancer, and soluble fiber has been proven to lower the incidence of heart disease. Legumes contain both, in a proportion of approximately 75% insoluble to 25% soluble.

Legumes are also some of the best natural sources of folate, the form of folic acid in foods. Folic acid has recently been making headlines for its role in reducing the incidence of coronary artery disease by lowering the level of an amino acid called homocysteine. In high concentrations, homocysteine promotes atherosclerosis. In addition, folic acid is essential in a healthy pregnancy to prevent birth defects.

Of all plants, legumes are tops in both the quantity and quality of protein. A half cup serving contains seven to eight grams of protein. Proteins are made up of amino acids. Amino acids are the building blocks with which to make proteins. Proteins are essential for all living organisms—plant or animal. There are twenty-two amino acids, of which fourteen are manufactured within our bodies. The other eight amino acids have to be obtained from our diet. They are called essential amino acids, because it is essential we get them from our diet. If a food's protein contains all eight essential amino acids it is called a complete protein. If it contains less than eight of the essential amino acids, it is called an incomplete protein. All animal meat, dairy products, and eggs contain complete protein. Grains, legumes, nuts, and seeds contain incomplete proteins. The only known exception at this time is soybeans, which contains complete protein.

Essential Amino Acids:
Tryptophan
Leucin
Isoleucin
Lysine
Valine
Threonine
Methionine
Phenylalanine

This fact has been misunderstood and misused to encourage people to eat more meat to get the complete proteins. However, this is not necessary. Plant proteins are often complementary, meaning one plant contains the essential amino acids that another does not. So, by eating the two plants you would get a complete protein. A perfect example is grains and legumes. Many grains are low in the essential amino acid lysine, but beans are high in lysine. Eaten together, they provide a complete protein.

God, of course, designed plants this way, since all people were vegetarians until the great flood. No one suffered from protein malnutrition during this time period as a result of their diet. In fact, if you think of it, where do the animals get their amino acids to make the complete protein? From their diet, which is vegetarian, for the majority of our meat food sources.

The health benefits of beans and other legumes are plentiful. In addition to their insoluble fiber lowering the risk of colon cancer and preventing constipation, their soluble fiber lowers cholesterol, improves blood sugar control, and lessens the risk of heart disease and diabetes. Fiber is turning out to be a major dietary method of lowering blood sugar. Fiber has also been shown to reduce insulin requirements in both type 1 and type 2 diabetics.

We already mentioned the benefit of folic acid found in legumes in the reduction of heart disease risk. In addition, legumes contain a wide variety of phytonutrients, including saponins, which bind with cholesterol and help eliminate it from the body. Red beans contain some of the same phytonutrients (called flavonoids) found in red grapes, so eating a cup of cooked red beans may have the same health benefits as drinking red wine or grape juice, namely, improving cholesterol profiles.

I know many readers are thinking, "Okay, I'm convinced beans are an important component of our diet, but they cause too much gas and are hard to digest". There are two reasons for this. First, beans, as already described, are very high in fiber, and when we suddenly increase fiber intake, we can experience some gastrointestinal problems. The keys to overcoming this problem are to slowly increase fiber intake to give your system time to adjust, and to be persistent. After a few days or weeks, your system will adapt to the high fiber and will, in fact, function much better as a result.

The second cause of gastrointestinal problems with beans is attributed to the types of sugar found in beans, which are called oligosaccharides. Beans contain two of these complex sugars called raffinose and stachyose. Our bodies lack the enzyme to digest them, but God took care of this problem as well. Living in our intestinal tract are friendly bacteria that digest these sugars for us. The problem is, if you have not been eating many legumes, the number of these good bacteria may be quite low. Once you start eating legumes on a regular (hopefully daily) basis, the number of these bacteria will increase and digest the sugars. Again, it may take a few days to a few weeks for this to happen, depending on your original number of bacteria. This is a good reason to avoid broad spectrum antibiotics if at all possible, because they kill the good bacteria as well as the bad.

There are some things you can do to eliminate a lot of the gastrointestinal problems associated with eating legumes, at least initially, until your body gets accustomed to legumes, as previously described.

The first is to "quick soak" the beans. This is accomplished by adding cleaned (dried) beans to boiling water and boiling them hard for two minutes, then turning off the stove to allow the beans to soak until they are fully rehydrated (no longer look shriveled). This usually takes two to four hours, depending on the type and size of the beans. Before you finish cooking the beans, pour off the water in which they soaked. This removes most of the oligosaccharides that cause gas formation. Add fresh water and cook the beans until they are done.

Another option is to use a product such as Beano with each serving of beans, which provides the enzyme needed to digest the complex sugars.

EZEKIEL BREAD

In the book of Ezekiel, God told Ezekiel, whom He had called to be a prophet to the Jewish nation exiled in Babylon, to lay on his left side for 390 consecutive days (one day for each year that the house of Israel had sinned against God) and then on his right side for forty days (one day for each year that the house of Judah had sinned against God). During this time, he was only to eat a special bread, for which God provided the recipe, and drink water. **"Take wheat and barley, beans and lentils, millet and spelt, put them in a storage jar and use them to make bread for yourself," Ezekiel 4:9.**

Spelt is an ancient grain that has been traced back as far as 5000 B.C. in the area we now call Iran. It has a nutty taste.

Millet is another grain. Today, it is well known as bird food, but it is very nutritious for human consumption. (But don't eat the bird food, it is not food grade!) Millet is low in starch and very high in protein. It is excellent to cook into a porridge and eat for breakfast. It can also be used to replace rice in rice recipes.

Ezekiel bread has been analyzed and found to contain all the essentials for health, including complete proteins.

This bread provided every essential element Ezekiel needed to stay healthy for 430 days. Only God could have known this during Ezekiel's time. Ezekiel bread serves as a perfect example of plants complementing each other to meet our nutritional needs.

NUTS AND SEEDS

Nuts are elaborate seeds and thus are included with the seed-bearing plants. For years, health authorities did not highly recommend eating nuts because of their high fat content. With the exception of chestnuts, about 50-75% of a nut's total calories come from fat. However, nuts contain mostly unsaturated fat, including oleic acid (a monosaturated fat). This kind of fat is not bad for you—the "bad" kinds of fat are called saturated and trans-saturated fat. The mostly monosaturated fat found in nuts has been shown to lower bad (LDL) cholesterol, lower blood pressure, and lower the risk of clogged arteries (atherosclerosis).

Nuts are also a wonderful source of arginine, an amino acid that is converted in your body to nitrous oxide, a substance that relaxes, or dilates, blood vessels and prevents blood clots. In addition, walnuts have substantial amounts of alpha-linolenic acid, an omega-3 fatty acid that has been shown to protect against heart disease.

Scientists have only recently discovered these amazing health benefits of nuts, but God told man to eat nuts around 6000 years ago. Does the scientific evidence support the health benefits of eating nuts?

According to data from the Physicians Health Study of 21,454 men, those men who ate nuts two or more times a week had only half the risk of dying from a heart-related event than men who rarely ate nuts, even after adjusting for other risk factors and habits (AIM 2002).

Researchers from Pennsylvania State University reviewed sixteen major studies and found that eating one ounce of nuts more than five times a week could reduce the risk of heart disease by 25-39%. In the Nurses Health Study of 86,000 women, researchers found that those who ate more than half a cup of nuts per week were 35% less likely to develop heart disease or suffer a heart attack than women who rarely ate nuts. Even those women who only ate nuts once a week had a 25% less risk of heart disease.

In addition, the Women's Health Study recently suggested that higher nut and even peanut butter consumption may lower the risk of type 2 diabetes. This benefit may be due to the unsaturated fat's ability to stabilize blood sugar and insulin levels.

Brazil nuts are extremely high in selenium and the phytonutrients quercetin and campferol, all of which have anti-cancer properties.

Despite nut's high fat content, they may even be useful as a diet aid to lose weight, if eaten in moderation to replace another high fat or protein food, since they are very filling.

Other seeds, such as sunflower and pumpkin seeds, may have similar beneficial properties to nuts but do not have the long term studies to prove it.

Endnotes

[1] *insulin* - a hormone secreted by the pancreas to regulate blood sugar levels

[2] *hyperlipidemia* - high blood levels of cholesterol, triglycerides or both

Chapter Five:
Fruits and Vegetables

Men who eat three servings a week of cruciferous vegetables reduce their risk of prostate cancer by 41%.

The second food source listed in **Genesis 1:29 is the "fruit with seed in it"**. This encompasses all fruit grown on trees, vines, and bushes, but also many of what are today classified as vegetables; including tomatoes, peppers, eggplants, squash, cucumbers, and okra. The third food source listed in **Genesis 1:30 is "every green plant"**. This includes most of the other vegetables.

Since very few studies look at the health benefits of just fruit or just vegetables, we will look at these two food sources as a single group. A person needs five to nine servings a day of a variety of different fruits and vegetables to meet our health needs. It is easier for me to remember that, on average, a person needs seven servings per day. As we studied in Chapter Three on phytonutrients, the brighter or darker colored produce contains the most nutrients, and in order to get different nutrients, we need to choose different colored produce.

Despite this knowledge, American consumers are doing just the opposite. Not only are we eating less produce, we are eating fewer varieties of produce. According to the USDA (United States Department of Agriculture), half of all the vegetables eaten in the U.S. in 1996 came from only three plants: lettuce (mostly Iceberg), potatoes, and tomatoes. In addition, just two kinds of peas account for 96% of the U.S. harvest.

In regards to fruit, Americans today eat less fruit than Americans in 1929, despite the fact that fruit is much more readily available today, and can be purchased in a much broader variety. Similar to the American consumption of vegetables, half of all fruit servings in 1996 came from only four fruits. World-wide, only fifteen species of plants and eight species of livestock account for 90% of all global food production.

Only one in four Americans today gets five servings of fruits and vegetables per day. Certainly, on our nutritional report card we must give ourselves an "F" for "failing".

You reap what you eat

Nutritionally, fresh fruits and vegetables are best, with frozen produce coming in at a close second. Raw is better than cooked, but any kind of fruit or vegetable is better than none at all. Organically grown fruits and vegetables are higher in nutrients, taste better, and do not have dangerous chemicals, such as insecticides or pesticides, on them.

When vegetables or fruit are cooked, use as little water as possible, since many of the nutrients in the food are water soluble and will leach out into the water they are cooked in. When possible, incorporate this water into your diet as a stock for soup or as a vegetable "gravy". (I love pouring the liquid from boiled cabbage over cornbread). The best way to cook vegetables is to conserve nutrients by steaming. Other excellent ways to cook them are grilling or stir frying. Cook vegetables only until they are "al dente," or are tender but still crisp. This gives vegetables the best taste and also retains more of their nutritional value.

"The closer a food is to the state in which it grows, the healthier it is"

NUTRITIONAL BENEFITS OF FRUITS AND VEGETABLES

The scientific evidence supporting the role of fruits and vegetables in preventing disease is so extensive it would be impractical to attempt to discuss it all. This discussion will include only a brief summary for some of the more common diseases.

Remember that the health benefits of fruits and vegetables are due to their phytonutrients, vitamins, and trace minerals. As a result, you cannot gain the same health benefits by taking nutritional supplements. No pill can compare to eating the actual food. As a result, think of food as God's medicine. This mindset offers several advantages. First, if you think of food as medicine, you may be more motivated to eat your seven servings of fruits and vegetables a day, even if you do not particularly like them. If a doctor prescribed a pill for you to take seven times a day, and told you the pill could prevent heart attacks, strokes, cancer, and diabetes, I believe that you would take it.

A second advantage to thinking of food as medicine is that it helps to control the quantity that we eat. We all know that just because a little medicine is good for you, a lot of medicine is not necessarily better. In fact, we know that the reality is just the opposite: too much medicine can be very harmful. Similarly, God's medicine is very beneficial to us, but eating in excess can cause deleterious results, such as obesity. Realize that you do not have to eat a lot of a particular food to gain its benefits.

A third advantage of the "food is medicine" mindset relates to our response to eating a food we do not particularly like. We often tell our children that when taking a medicine that tastes bad, they need to take it anyway, because it is good for them. So do you! If a food offers lots of health benefits, but you do not like it, make yourself take a few bites. Repeat this effort every few days, and you will acquire a taste for it. Remember, you do not have to eat a lot of "medicine" for it to be beneficial to you.

"Our food should be our medicine and our medicine should be our food."
-Hippocrates
~400 BC

The fourth and final advantage is that this mindset adds a whole new perspective on "saying grace" before we eat. If we are eating foods that God told us to eat, and that we know contain medicine to prevent disease from coming upon us, **we can truly be thankful that God provided us with this food**, and ask him to bless it to our bodies. However, if we are eating food that God forbade or that we know is harmful to our health (no matter how good it tastes or how much we are craving it), how hypocritical it is to thank God for those foods and how audacious we would be to ask Him to bless that food to our bodies.

"So whether you eat or drink, or whatever you do, do it all for the glory of God."
-I Corinthians 10:31

Remember this as we look at the proven health benefits of fruits and vegetables. Commit to God that you will incorporate these foods into your diet and then expect Him to truly bless your health.

The number one cause of death in our country is atherosclerotic cardiovascular disease (ASCVD). This is commonly referred to as "hardening of the arteries". It is due to plaque buildup inside the arteries that leads to narrow or stenotic areas that can then completely occlude, resulting in heart attacks or strokes. There are many things that increases a person's risk of developing ASCVD, including smoking, obesity, high cholesterol, high blood pressure, diabetes, elevated [1]**homocysteine** levels, and even a family history of ASCVD.

What you do not know can kill you. "My people are destroyed for lack of knowledge"-Hosea 4:6

On the other hand, your choice of lifestyle can dramatically reduce your risk of developing ASCVD. Do not smoke, and if you do, quit. If you are overweight, lose weight by starting a regular exercise program and changing your diet to the Bible diet.

Dutch researchers recently reviewed the findings of twelve studies that looked at the benefits of eating whole foods instead of vitamin supplements and concluded that eating the fruits and vegetables could reduce the risk of heart disease by 20-40%. How do they accomplish this?

Many fruits and vegetables are high in soluble fiber, which helps lower cholesterol. Canadian researchers conducted a small study placing thirteen men and women on a diet rich in fruits and vegetables, along with soy burgers, oatmeal, almonds, and beans. After one month, blood levels of LDL (the "bad" cholesterol) had fallen by 29%, a drop similar to that seen with prescription statin medications (Metabolism, December 2002).

The Dietary Approach to Stop Hypertension (DASH) study has proven that eating eight to ten servings of fruit and vegetables a day lowers blood pressure. A Harvard University study showed that a vegetarian diet could lower blood pressure by 15% in just two weeks (as well as most blood pressure medications). This blood pressure reduction effect may be due to the magnesium and potassium in fruits and vegetables as well as phytonutrients. Fruits and vegetables may also produce a diuretic effect by promoting salt excretion.

The folate and vitamin B6 found in produce help lower blood levels of homocysteine. Homocysteine is an amino acid that, when present at high levels, leads to atherosclerosis. Many vegetables have [1]**anti-platelet** effects similar to aspirin, or actually contain salicylic acid, which is the active ingredient in aspirin. This helps prevent blood clot formations that can cause heart attacks or strokes.

Lycopene is a phytonutrient found in tomatoes, pink grapefruit, strawberries, watermelon, and other pink-tinted fruits and vegetables. A Harvard study of 28,000 women showed that those with the highest lycopene levels were only half as likely to develop heart disease over five years as those with the lowest levels.

In addition, fruits and vegetables play a major role in weight management because they are low in calories in their natural state. Fruits and vegetables can be eaten fairly freely **as long as they are not excessively sweetened or covered with high fat toppings like cheese sauce, butter or margarine, sour cream, or bacon bits.**

"The closer a food is to the state in which it grows, the healthier it is"

In regards to preventing strokes, called cerebrovascular accidents (CVA), vegetables and fruits also are dietary heroes. In a Japanese study called the Life Span Study, involving nearly 40,000 participants, those who ate fruits and green-yellow vegetables almost daily were **approximately 20-40% less likely to suffer a fatal stroke** of any kind than those eating these foods less than once a week. The protective effect was seen in both types of stroke ([2]ischemic and [3]hemorrhagic) and was similar in men and women. This benefit may be due to the vitamin C, beta carotene, and other antioxidants which guard against plaque buildup in arteries, as well as potassium and magnesium's abilities to lower blood pressure and by fiber's ability to lower cholesterol and blood sugar levels.

"You reap what you eat."

The second leading cause of death in America is cancer. It is now known that 60% of all cancers are related to diet, including cancer of the esophagus, stomach, colon, prostate, bladder, and skin. The American Institute for Cancer Research (AICR) estimates that eating a diet containing substantial amounts of a variety of fruits and vegetables can prevent at least 20% of all cancers.

My people are destroyed for lack of knowledge"
-Hosea 4:6

Studies have shown that 90% of all colon cancer can be linked to dietary and lifestyle factors, such as sedentary habits (increases risk) versus regular exercise (lowers risk). The strongest dietary protectors against colon cancer are vegetables, especially those high in folate, such as green leafy vegetables, and citrus fruits, like oranges. A few other dietary super heroes in the prevention of cancer are tomatoes and the cruciferous vegetables (cabbage, broccoli, cauliflower, brussels sprouts, and kale).

Tomatoes contain the phytonutrient lycopene, which has been shown to have anti-cancer properties. Cooking tomatoes makes the lycopene more available, so the best sources are tomato paste or sauce, canned tomatoes, and stewed tomatoes.

A Harvard study of 48,000 men showed that men who ate tomato sauce two or more times a week lowered their risk of prostate cancer by 36% over a twelve year period, compared with those men who ate less than one serving a month. Another study, however, showed that it is not just the lycopene, but the whole tomato that exerts the anti-cancer benefit. An Ohio State University animal study treated 194 rats with drugs to induce prostate cancer and fed the rats either dried whole tomato powder, pure lycopene, or a placebo for fourteen months. The whole tomato powder group was 26% less likely to die from prostate cancer than the placebo group, but the lycopene supplement group fared only slightly better than the placebo group.

In regard to cruciferous vegetables, individuals who eat seven or more servings per week have one half the risk of bladder cancer. A study done at the Fred Hutchison Cancer Research Center in Seattle showed that men who ate three servings a week of cruciferous vegetables reduced their risk of prostate cancer by 41%.

Other benefits of fruits and vegetables include reducing the risk of asthma, [4]emphysema, and chronic bronchitis secondary to their antioxidant properties, according to a study at Cornell University. Five or more servings a day significantly reduces the development of actinic keratosis (pre-cancerous lesions of the skin) as well as actual skin cancers.

Leafy green vegetables lower the risk of [5]osteoporosis because they contain vitamin K, which is necessary to make a protein essential for normal bone formation.

Dark green leafy vegetables, as well as other vegetables rich in the phytonutrients carotenoid including lutein and zeaxanthin protect against age related macular degeneration—the most common cause of permanent vision loss in the elderly. The risk of having age related macular degeneration is decreased by nearly half by increasing carotenoids in your diet. In addition, researchers have shown that individuals who eat more than one and a half servings of fruits and vegetables a day are five times less likely to develop cataracts.

Fruits and vegetables also stimulate the immune system by providing antioxidants (vitamins A, C, and E, beta carotene, selenium, and zinc) and by supplying vitamin B6, folate, copper, iron, and magnesium—all of which are necessary for a healthy immune system to fight infection and attack cancer cells.

Fruits and vegetables rich in vitamin C protect against gallstones. Studies reveal that those individuals with the highest vitamin C intake had half the risk of gallstones compared to those with moderate vitamin C intake. Another phytonutrient contained in cruciferous vegetables, sulforaphane, may even prevent stomach ulcers. Sulforaphane has been shown to kill Heliobacter pylori, a bacteria that is thought to cause stomach ulcers.

Thus, you can see that **there are great health benefits to be gained by eating just seven servings a day of a variety of fruits and vegetables.** Truly, this is God's medicine, and we should commit to getting our seven servings every day just as zealously as if we were taking a prescribed pill.

Endnotes

1. ***anti-platelet*** - keeps blood platelets from sticking together and forming clots
   The closer a food is to the state in which it grows, the healthier it is.
   You reap what you eat
2. ***Ischemic*** - loss of blood supply due to a clot or hardening of the arteries
3. ***hemorrhagic*** - bleeding into an organ resulting in damage to the tissue
4. ***Emphysema*** - a chronic lung disease usually seen in smokers
5. ***Osteoporosis*** - softening of bones that frequently occurs with aging.

Chapter Six:
...all the fat is the Lord's
– Leviticus 3:16

It should be noted that for the first 2000 or so years after Creation, men were strict vegetarians (herbivores). It was not until after the great flood that God gave man permission to eat meat. In fact, it was not just man, but all animals that were vegetarians during these first 2000 years. **"To every beast of the earth, to every bird of the air, and to everything that creeps on the earth, in which there is life, I have given every green herb for food" (Genesis 1:30).**

There is no direct evidence to indicate when some of the animals became meat eaters (carnivores), but it would make sense that this also occurred after the flood for several reasons. The Bible does not record that Noah took any meat on board the ark to use as a food supply for any of the animals. This might also explain why Noah had no fear of any of the animals, and why they had no fear of him. In addition, although God had already denoted some animals as clean and others as unclean **(Genesis 7:2)**, man was not yet forbidden to eat any of the animals. After the flood, it is written in **Genesis 9:2-4, "And the fear of you and the dread of you shall be upon every beast of the earth, and upon every fowl of the air, upon all that moveth upon the earth, and upon the fishes of the sea; into your hands are they delivered. Every moving thing that liveth shall be meat for you, even as the green herb have I given you all things. But flesh with the life thereof, which is the blood thereof, shall you not eat."**

In other words, man was allowed to eat any animal that lived upon the earth at this time. The reason for this may well be because no animals were carnivorous yet, and thus there had not been time for their flesh to be tainted. This would make sense when we see that all carnivorous animals were revealed to Moses as unclean. What do I mean by their flesh being tainted?

This all relates to the curse that fell upon the earth as a result of Adam and Eve's sin **(Genesis 3:16-19)**. We see many changes that fell upon man as time evolved because of the curse. For example, it was initially acceptable for relatives to marry because there were no genetic defects at that time. All DNA was perfect, as was everything God had created: **"And God saw everything He had made, and behold, it was very good—suitable, pleasant—and He approved it completely" (Genesis 1:31)**. Since all DNA was perfect, there was no concern about relatives having similar genetic defects, which could result in birth defects and inherited diseases. But as time went on, as a result of the curse, genetic defects started to occur and God told Moses to forbid people who were related from marrying each other.

Similarly, just after the flood, all meat was fit for human consumption, but as time went on, some meat, revealed to Moses as "unclean" animals, became unfit for human consumption. All scavengers and land-dwelling carnivores became unclean animals. What happened? Most likely as disease became more prevalent in the world and as pollutions, toxins, and poisons accumulated, animals (including humans) started getting sicker and dying earlier. We know that toxins and poisons are stored in fat and many infections (especially parasites) occur in the flesh and thus, carnivores, by eating sick, weak, or dead animals, accumulated the toxins and poisons that were in the animals they ate and acquired their diseases. Therefore, each generation of carnivores got more and more tainted until, by the time of Moses (and most likely a little before), carnivores were unfit for human consumption.

This brings us to the Mosaic law regarding meat consumption recorded in Leviticus 11 and Deuteronomy 14. But before we get to these specific statutes concerning which animals to eat and not eat, we must look at a more general law that is of utmost importance to our health. This law is found in **Leviticus 3:17, "This is a lasting ordinance for the generations to come, wherever you live: You must not eat any fat or blood."** There are at least nineteen different Hebrew and Aramaic words used in the Old Testament that can be translated as fat. The interpretations of the different words vary from literal fat or suet to figurative rich, fertile, choicest, or valuable, and there are even words for obesity, olive oil, and a verb for "to be stupid". As you see, there are many words that can be read as fat, the meaning depending upon the word used and the context in which it is used.

The word used in Leviticus 3:17 and in Leviticus 7:23 (which will be discussed later), is **"cheleb"**, which was the word used to specifically describe the fat that is located around the kidneys and liver. This is the fat from which animal shortening or lard is derived: it was the choicest fat, the most desirable, and so the most appropriate as a sacrifice for God. We read in **Leviticus 3:14-16, "From what he offers he is to make this offering to the Lord by fire: all the fat that covers the inner parts or is connected to them, both kidneys with the fat on them near the loins, and the covering of the liver, which he will remove with the kidneys. The priest shall burn them on the altar as food, an offering made by fire, a pleasing aroma. All the fat is the Lord's."**

We see, then, that all the fat in certain animals was to be set aside as a sacrifice unto God and was absolutely not to be eaten. **Leviticus 7:25 says, "Anyone who eats the fat of an animal from which an offering by fire may be made to the Lord must be cut off from his people"**, illustrating a very stiff penalty for disobeying God.

Which animals are being referred to here? **Leviticus 7:23** clarifies the issue, **"Do not eat any of the fat of cattle, sheep, or goats."** We see that the fat being referred to is the fat from what we refer to today as red meat. Today we call this fat suet, from which we get animal shortening or lard, which is a saturated fat.

Today, it is well established that saturated fat is the one component of our diet that contributes the most to preventable disease. Saturated fat is the major dietary cause of atherosclerosis, the hardening of the arteries that leads to heart attacks and strokes. Saturated fat intake has also been shown to be a major contributor to breast, colon, prostate, bladder, and uterine cancers as well as some types of lymphoma. Saturated fat also weakens the immune system and our ability to fight infections. How amazing is it that, approximately 3500 years ago, Moses forbade the children of Israel to eat the fat of red meat? How could Moses have known this if the knowledge had not been given to him by God?

The second requirement of Leviticus 3:17 is a repeat of what God told Noah in Genesis 9:4—not to eat any meat with its lifeblood still in it. In this verse, we see that this is a lasting (or perpetual) ordinance, including mankind today. This is stated again in **Leviticus 7:26, "And wherever you live, you must not eat the blood of any bird or animal. If anyone eats blood, that person must be cut off from his people."**

The Bible specifies that when an animal was slain, its neck was to be cut and the blood drained from its body. The blood was to be sprinkled on the altar and burned along with the fat as an offering unto God. The Bible also clearly points out the reason for this from a spiritual standpoint. The blood is the life force of the animal. God tells us that the penalty of sin is death. The death and sacrifice of the animal, represented by its blood and fat, was to be presented to God as a burnt offering to atone for man's sins.

There are two interesting points to be made here. First, Noah and Moses both knew that the blood was the source of life to the animal, something not known by the scientific community until William Harvey's work on the circulatory system in 1628, more than 3000 years later. Obviously, this advanced knowledge had to come from God. Secondly, as in the case for fat (in that saturated fat has been shown to be very unhealthy), there is a physical benefit as well as a spiritual reason for avoiding blood. Recent outbreaks of E. coli infections, mad cow disease, and many other blood borne diseases remind us of the necessity in following this law. Be sure all meat is cooked until well done and avoid gravies made from meat drippings (which are fat and blood).

Another very important concept to remember is that eating fat and blood was not only forbidden for all generations, but to do otherwise was specified to be a sin. **I Samuel 2:12-17** tells a story of Eli's (the high priest) sons, who were disobeying God's orders in the handling of the Lord's offering. The Bible says, "This sin of the young men was very great in the Lord's sight, for they were treating the Lord's offering with contempt." What was their sin? They were eating meat with the fat still on it.

Similarly, in **1 Samuel 14:32-33**, the famished Israelites were eating uncooked meat after battling the Philistines all day and killing some of the captured livestock. **Verse 33** says, **"Then someone said to Saul, 'Look, the men are sinning against the Lord by eating meat that has blood in it.'"**

Finally, God reveals through Ezekiel one of the reasons that the Israelites lost the promised land and were taken into captivity: **"Since you eat meat with the blood still in it and look to your idols and shed blood, should you then possess the land?" (Ezekiel 33:25)**. God placed eating meat with the blood still in it on the same level as worshiping idols and committing murder! Eating the fat of red meat and eating meat with its blood still in it were sins in the eyes of the Lord.

Note, however, that man is not forbidden to eat all fat, just the fat from red meat. And, we are not forbidden to eat the fat that is marbled throughout the meat. Although it should certainly speak to us about the quantity of red meat we eat, and I believe it speaks to the fact that we should trim all fat off the meat before it is cooked. Similarly, we are not forbidden to eat vegetable fat (oil), but we know there are some vegetable oils better than others, nor are we forbidden to eat the fat in nuts or white meat.

This is an important distinction, since for several years, Americans were encouraged to follow a low fat diet, which we discovered did not work very well. The dieters were not any healthier and most actually gained weight. Thus, we realized that the body needs some fat, and that the fat found in nuts, fish, olives, and some other vegetable oils are actually healthy and necessary for normal bodily function. Again, in complete agreement to what God told Moses.

The relationship of fat (both the type and amount of fat) was studied by French researchers in the Lyon Diet Heart Study. These researchers took 605 people who had had a previous heart attack and put half of them on the American Heart Association (AHA) diet and half on the Mediterranean diet.

The AHA diet is lower in total fat but also lower in plant foods and higher in animal products, and thus saturated fat.

The Mediterranean diet has changed very little from Jesus's day and closely resembles the Bible diet. It is rich in fruits, vegetables, whole grains, legumes, fish, and olive oil. This diet is higher in total fat than the AHA diet, but contains less animal fat and more monosaturated fat (the good fat found in nuts, fish, olive oil, and other plant based oils).

After four years, those on the Mediterranean diet had a staggering 50-70% less risk of repeat heart attacks than those on the AHA diet, despite similar blood pressure and cholesterol levels. Furthermore, the study also showed those on the Mediterranean diet had a lower risk of cancer and were less likely to die of any cause than those on the AHA diet.

Why does the type of fat make a difference? To understand this we need to examine the types of fats in our diet. The four main kinds of fats are monosaturated fats, polyunsaturated fats, saturated fats, and trans-saturated fats.

The monosaturated fats are definitely the good fats you should include in your diet and are found in nuts, olives and olive oils, and fish. Some other vegetable oils are monosaturated, such as canola oil, but recent evidence indicates that when used for cooking purposes, trans-saturated fats are formed in the canola oil. Olive oil is much more stable at high temperatures and thus a better choice to use when cooking.

Polyunsaturated fats are prevalent in most vegetable oils and may have some health benefits, but since they are also a prominent source of calories, consumption of these fats needs to be monitored.

Saturated fats we have already discussed, but I should point out that saturated fat is found in palm tree and coconut oils. Although not forbidden in the Bible, their use should probably be limited. This is important because many products on supermarket shelves have had coconut and/or palm tree oil added to them as a cheap source of fat to satisfy the consumer's "fat tooth". All saturated fat should be limited.

Trans-saturated fats do not occur in nature. They are formed when other fats are heated to high temperatures. The most common example of this is margarine. There are some margarines now that are "trans free," and if you eat margarine, this is certainly the kind you should eat. Trans-saturated fats are also common in crackers, french fries, potato chips, cookies, and pastries. Trans-saturated fats are probably worse than saturated fats in promoting disease. God did not warn Moses about trans-saturated fats because they did not exist at his time. All trans-saturated fats should be avoided.

"The closer a food is to the state in which it grows, the healthier it is"

To further understand the Lyon Diet Heart Study and dietary fats in general, we need to look at fat composition in more detail. The elements of fat that we must obtain from our diet are called fatty acids. Just as there are essential amino acids (see Chapter Four), there are also essential fatty acids. These are fat substances that our bodies cannot make and which must be supplied in our diet.

Fatty acids can be divided into three classes: omega-9 fatty acids, omega-6 fatty acids, and omega-3 fatty acids. Without these fatty acids, your body would simply shut down. We will now look at omega-6 and omega-3 fatty acids.

The omega-6 fatty acids include linoleic acid, gamma linolenic acid (GLA), and arachidonic acid. The omega-3 fatty acids include alpha-linolenic acid (ALA), eicosapentaenoic acid (EPA), and docosahexaenoic acid (DHA). The omega-3 fatty acids have been most extensively studied in regards to their health benefits.

Research has shown that EPA helps reduce platelet aggregation, having a similar effect to aspirin. By preventing clot formation, EPA can help prevent plaque build-up, which leads to heart attacks and ischemic strokes. DHA, on the other hand, has been shown to stabilize heart rhythm, which is important in preventing irregular heartbeats in people recovering from heart attacks.

Foods rich in EPA, DHA, and ALA have also been shown to lower blood pressure and triglycerides. These fatty acids make up the monosaturated fats, and so are found in the same foods high in monosaturated fats. EPA and DHA are found only in seafood, and are especially plentiful in cold water fish like salmon, mackerel, tuna, and sardines. ALA is found in walnuts, flaxseed and some vegetable oils, such as canola and soybean. You also get some omega-3 fatty acids from spinach, mustard greens, and wheat germ. These foods contain linolenic acid, which is converted to EPA and DHA in the body, but not very efficiently. You must eat ten times more linolenic acid as EPA to get the same blood levels of EPA.

It is these omega-3 fatty acids and their beneficial effects on the heart that is believed to have produced the results of the Lyon Diet Heart Study. In addition, recent studies with omega-3 fatty acids have shown that they exert anti-inflammatory effects that can be used to treat kidney diseases and rheumatoid arthritis. They have also been found to have anti-cancer properties and seem to be essential for normal brain and central nervous system function.

The omega-6 fatty acids make up approximately 90% of the polyunsaturated fats in our diet and seem to have their largest influence on our health by producing a whole class of hormones called eicosanoids (omega-3 fatty acids form eicosanoids also).

Thus, we see that just as there are good and bad carbohydrates, there are also good and bad fats. And once again, modern science has shown that the type beneficial to our health is the type God specifically told us to eat.

Some of you at this time may be thinking the same thought many of my patients have expressed over the years: "If eating fat is so bad for you, why did my grandparents get by with eating fat like bacon, sausage, butter, and lard?"

First of all, our ancestors did not eat more fat than we do. Americans today consume twice as much (per individual, not per capita) butter, shortening, oil, and sugar, than our counterparts in 1909. Furthermore, we consume (again, per person) seven and a half times more cheese, five times more chicken, 24% more beef, and 15% more pork than did Americans at the beginning of the 20th century (Discover, "Eat locally-think globally," May 2001). Let's face it, America has become a nation of gluttons, and as a result, the office of the Surgeon General reports that 60% of all adults in this country are overweight or obese.

Every year obesity accounts for 300,000 preventable deaths (second only to tobacco), and obesity related diseases cost the country 100 billion dollars a year. Diabetes has reached epidemic proportions in both adults and children as a result of this rise in obesity.

Just as you cannot violate God's spiritual laws without paying a penalty, you also cannot violate God's dietary laws without paying a penalty. In the case of his dietary laws, the penalty is that our physical health suffers. As I will show in the next chapter, we as a nation, and worst of all, as Christians, are in violation of many of God's dietary laws when it comes to meat consumption.

"It is only when we have learned to recognize that Gods law for the human body is as sacred as is God's law for the human soul, that we shall began to understand the religion of the heart."
Religion of Health by Elizabeth Blackwell.

Chapter Seven:
Is all meat clean?

God's dietary laws governing our meat consumption are simple and very precise, yet often misunderstood and almost always controversial. Why are the laws controversial? The main controversy is whether these Old Testament laws still apply to us today. We have seen how relevant God's first three dietary laws are to our health, i.e., the seed bearing plants, the fruit bearing plants, and every green plant where the plant itself is the primary food source.

Having shown how healthy God's dietary laws concerning plants are, why would we not have the same confidence and expectation concerning God's dietary laws for animals?

Nevertheless, I was taught that the New Testament revealed we no longer needed to be concerned about these laws. I was taught that the laws did not apply to us today because of grace: since we are saved under grace, we are no longer bound to the law. I believe this concept is misunderstood. I believe we are getting confused between what is spiritually permissible and what is physically wise.

Most of the dietary meat laws are found in Leviticus 11 and Deuteronomy 14. The first step in understanding these laws is to know the context in which they were written. These books-Leviticus and Deuteronomy-contain many other laws or statutes that deals with day to day life. They start with dietary laws but then proceed to discuss laws dealing with contamination by touching dead carcasses, or by dead animals and reptiles coming into contact with their cooking vessels, waterpots, or seeds to plant into the garden. There are laws that deal with child birth, infectious skin diseases, and bodily discharges. There are even laws that deal with mildew on clothing and in homes. There are sanitation laws requiring the people to go outside the camp to relieve themselves, including digging a hole and burying their excrement (Deuteronomy 23:12-13). Other laws regarded quarantine and washing of the hands and clothing after handling the dead (Numbers 19), handling unclean food (Leviticus 11:29-40)., and not eating roadkill (Deuteronomy 14:21).

Although I believe that there may be some spiritual lessons to be learned from these rules and regulations, it seem obvious that predominantly these laws are for medical or health purposes. I believe the same can be said about the dietary laws concerning meat. They were given to Moses by God to show us what to eat and what not to eat in order to maintain excellent health.

Furthermore, since these rules and regulations were given to Moses by God, they represent divine wisdom. Only God knew, at the time of Moses, that germs existed and transmitted disease. All the Mosaic laws concerning washing of hands, quarantining of the sick, and burying waste products made no sense whatsoever without a knowledge of how disease was transmitted. The Israelites had to accept these rules by faith. Since it is obvious these laws and the knowledge they represented must have come from God, we can be equally sure they are for our own good. Because, who knows better what we should and should not eat than our Creator? If this diet was best for people in Moses's time, would it not still be best for us today? Does God or His wisdom change? **"Jesus Christ is the same yesterday and today and forever," Hebrews 13:8.** Therefore, if these dietary laws are based on God's divine wisdom, and if His wisdom never changes, it seems obvious that we should still be following these rules today. So where is the controversy?

The controversy arises in several New Testament passages that seem, at first inspection, to negate the need to follow God's dietary rules. In order to understand what these scriptures were referring to, we must understand some of the events taking place at the time they were written.

The early Jewish Christians struggled with decisions concerning whether the Gentiles had to adopt Jewish laws in order to become members of the early church. These debates specifically concerned whether the Gentiles had to be circumcised (per Jewish tradition) and whether they had to accept the Jewish dietary laws in order to become Christians.

Another debate the early Christians were struggling with was whether it was permissible to eat meat that had been sacrificed to false idols by the Romans. Meat was very scarce at the time, and most of the meat sold in the markets came from animals that had been sacrificed to false gods.

A third problem centered around the fact that there were false teachers in the early churches that were putting unnecessary requirements on becoming a Christian, including vigorous physical exercise, forbidding people to marry, and ordering people to abstain from certain foods (even clean foods). Now let us look at some of these New Testament passages to see their full meaning.

The passage singled out most frequently to support the viewpoint that all foods are okay to eat is Peter's vision, described in Acts 10:1-35. Many readers may be familiar with the passage, but in summary, Peter had a vision in which he saw heaven opened and something like a large sheet being let down to earth by its four corners. It contained all kinds of four-footed animals, as well as reptiles of the earth and birds of the air. Then a voice told him, **"Get up, Peter. Kill and eat." "Surely not, Lord!"** Peter replied, **"I have never eaten anything impure or unclean."** The voice spoke to him a second time, **"Do not call anything impure that God has made clean."** This happened three times, and immediately the sheet was taken back to heaven.

The Bible tells us Peter wondered about the meaning of the vision. If the vision pertained to clean and unclean animals, there would have been no reason to wonder about its meaning. However, two days later in the house of Cornelius (a Gentile), while addressing a large group of people, Peter said, **"You are well aware that it is against our law for a Jew to associate with a Gentile** or visit him. But God has shown me that I should not call any man impure or unclean." The vision, therefore, was not about clean and unclean animals, but about men, and what the Jews believed concerning Gentiles being unclean. This vision convinced the early Christians to extend the Gospel to the Gentiles.

Another passage is found in **Mark 7:5-23**. Jesus and his followers were being criticized for eating food with unwashed hands. The religious establishment of the Jews taught this was a sin. Jesus pointed out the hypocrisy of their teachings and ended his discourse with the statement, **"Listen to me, everyone, and understand this. Nothing outside a man can make him 'unclean' by going into him. Rather, it is what comes out of a man that makes him 'unclean'." Later, Jesus said to his disciples, "Don't you see that nothing that enters a man from the outside can make him 'unclean'? For it doesn't go into his heart, but into his stomach, and then out of his body." (In saying this, Jesus declared all foods "clean".) He went on: "What comes out of a man is what makes him 'unclean'. For from within, out of men's hearts, come evil thoughts, sexual immorality, theft, murder, adultery, greed, malice, deceit, lewdness, envy, slander, arrogance, and folly. All of these evils come from inside and make a man "unclean".**

Obviously, in this passage, Jesus is referring to what is spiritually clean and unclean. He is clearly saying that eating food, any food, is not what makes a man spiritually unclean. He is not saying that all foods are okay to eat and are healthy for us. He is not saying that it is okay to eat unclean animals. If He was, then in essence, He would be saying that God had changed His laws, but we know theologically that God cannot change. In addition, if Jesus believed it was okay to eat unclean animals, He would have done so at some point in time during his ministry. Why do I believe this? Jesus was constantly pointing out to the Pharisees the difference between God's laws and man's traditions. If it was only a tradition (such as the ceremonial washing of hands prior to meals) to avoid unclean animals, then Jesus would have pointed that out by violating the tradition. How do I know He didn't? Jesus was constantly being watched by the religious establishment to see when He violated any Jewish tradition to prove He was a false prophet. If Jesus had ever eaten an unclean animal, it would have created a major disturbance, and it certainly would have been recorded in the Bible or Jewish Talmud, but it is not. Jesus was not saying there are no unclean animals—He was saying the food you eat is not what makes you righteous or unrighteous. It is not a spiritual issue, it is a physical issue. Also notice that the sentence, **"In saying this, Jesus declared all foods 'clean'" (verse 19b)**, is in parentheses in the NIV translation of the Bible. In the King James Version, this sentence is not present at all. The reason is that this sentence is not in the earliest Greek manuscripts and was added at a later time as a commentary and thus was placed in parentheses.

Other New Testament scriptures often misinterpreted or taken out of context are Colossians 2:16, 1 Timothy 4:4, and Romans 14:14. Let's look at each one of these in the context of the situation in which they occurred.

Colossians 2:16, "Therefore do not let anyone judge you by what you eat or drink," was said in reference to a controversy in the early church. Some believed that Gentiles could not become Christians unless they converted to Judaism and adopted all the Jewish traditions and laws and observed their religious festivals and ceremonies. Paul was simply saying in this verse that men should not be judged (again, we are talking spiritually here) by what they eat or by whether they are circumcised. He is not saying that we should eat anything we want, oblivious to God's dietary laws, or making a statement concerning the wisdom of doing so, but simply that it is not a requirement to be saved.

1 Timothy 4:4, "For everything God created is good, and nothing is to be rejected if it is received with thanksgiving, because it is consecrated by the word of God and prayer," was pertaining to a false teaching in the early church that restricted several things the believers were doing, including eating certain "clean" foods. History reveals that there were false teachers at the church of Ephesus. These were Greek philosophers who had been influenced by the church but were not willing to believe that Jesus was fully human. They believed that the body was evil, and added many restrictions to the Christian faith to make them appear self-disciplined, and thus, righteous. These restrictions included forbidding marriage, and abstaining from many foods, even foods listed as "clean" in the Mosaic laws. Paul was telling Timothy not to be fooled by these false teachings.

In Romans 14:14, Paul was speaking in regards to the controversy concerning whether to eat meat that had been sacrificed to false idols when he said, **"I am fully convinced that no food is unclean in itself"**. At the

Jerusalem council (Acts 15:19), Paul had agreed to send a letter to the Gentile churches requesting that they not eat meat that had been sacrificed to idols in order to prevent a rift in the early church. Now, talking to them in person, Paul is explaining his stance. Paul is saying, "Personally, I do not have a problem with you eating meat sacrificed to false idols as long as you know and worship the true God and give thanks to Him for the food. But don't do it if it offends a brother of weaker faith". His original stance at the Jerusalem council was based on his knowledge that many Jewish believers would be greatly offended by the Gentile believers eating this meat, and his fear was that this would create a division in the church.

The main message here is that man is not made unclean by what we eat, therefore, spiritually, whatever you choose to eat is okay (except for fat and blood). But none of these verses negate the need to follow God's dietary laws for health purposes. As Christians, we are free to eat whatever we want, but that does not mean that we should. **1 Corinthians 10:23 says, "Everything is permissible—but not everything is beneficial. Everything is permissible—but not everything is constructive."**

On the other hand, if we choose to consistently violate God's dietary laws to the detriment of our health, then it does become a spiritual issue.

Remember that we are the temple of the living God, that we are not our own, but were bought with a price, and therefore we are to honor God with our body. If it can be shown that eating the unclean foods is detrimental to our health and Paul says in **1 Corinthians 3:16, "Don't**

you know that you yourselves are God's temple and that God's spirit lives in you? If anyone destroys God's temple, God will destroy him; for God's temple is sacred and you are that temple", then it becomes clear that although we may be spiritually free to eat whatever we want, we are also spiritually obligated to follow God's dietary laws to keep our bodies as healthy as possible. Jesus did. Jesus said, **"I came not to do away with the law, but to fulfill it."** If God expected us to follow His dietary rules while under the law, how dare we not want to follow them while under grace? If God says these rules are for your health and your body is God's temple, which Jesus died for, how can we willfully and knowingly ignore God's dietary laws?

I hope I have convinced you that we should still be following God's dietary laws concerning meat. Now let's look at what those laws are.

Chapter Eight:

God's Dietary Laws Concerning Meat

People who eat fish just once a week have a 20-30% less risk of mouth, esophagus, stomach, pancreas, colon, and rectal cancers. Those who eat two or more servings per week have a 30-50% less risk of these same cancers.

God's regulations concerning meat consumption are recorded in Leviticus 11 and Deuteronomy 14.

In Leviticus 11:1 we read, "The Lord said to Moses and Aaron, 'say to the Israelites "of all the animals that live on land, these are the ones you may eat: you may eat any animal that has a split hoof completely divided and that chews the cud"'".

This rule allowed the consumption of cattle and sheep and today would includ venison. On the other hand, this restriction prevented the Jewish people from eating pork, since pigs have a split hoof, but don't chew the cud, and rabbits, which chew the cud but don't have a split hoof. The Bible says you must not eat any animal that only chews the cud or only has a split hoof—it must do both.

I have been taught that the spiritual significance of this passage is that "chewing the cud" represents meditating on the word of God and that "having a divided hoof" represents walking a separate walk from the rest of the world. The only way we as Christians can walk a separate walk is to meditate on the word of God daily, thus we must have a "divided hoof" and "chew the cud".

Throughout the Bible, God frequently has dual meanings for specific Bible passages—both a spiritual meaning as well as a more practical or physical meaning. Jesus used this technique also, as demonstrated in many of his parables, thus, I believe there is a practical, physical, and health related reason for not eating pork, rabbits, camels, etc., as well as having an underlying spiritual significance.

We already know that rabbits and pork carry diseases and parasites that other red meat does not but I believe there is more than that. I won't be surprised if someday we discover that there is something different about pork (and other forbidden meats), that make them unhealthy for us. Why am I confident of this fact? Because our Creator, who knows everything there is to know about our health, went to great effort and great detail to tell us NOT to eat these meats.

How about seafood? I'm getting ready to step on more toes. God said, **"Of all the creatures living in the water of the seas and the streams, you may eat any that have fins and scales. But all the creatures in**

the seas or streams that do not have fins or scales— you are to detest. And since you are to detest them; you must not eat their meat," Leviticus 11:9-11.

I love seafood, and I used to love shell fish. One day I got a bacterial dysentery from eating raw oysters—I believe that was God's first message to me that I was not to eat these animals for food. God's law in Leviticus 11:9-11 forbids us from eating oysters, crab meat, clams, lobsters, shrimp, mussels, and scallops. It also prohibits us from eating catfish, which have fins but no scales.

Why are we to detest them? I believe it is because of the curse. Remember, that as a result of the curse placed on the earth following Adam and Eve's fall from grace, death was introduced into the world (Romans 5:12). Because of disease and death, God had to convert some animals into scavengers to clean up the dead. Shellfish and catfish are scavengers and seeing them should remind us of their job, and that their job would not be necessary if man had not rebelled against God. Thus, we are to find them detestable.

Medically speaking, what is wrong with eating these forbidden animals? Scavengers live off carrion (dead and putrefying flesh). In doing so, they often incorporate disease and toxins into their own bodies, which are then passed on to us if we eat them. Catfish do this in lakes and ponds, eating the dead flesh that sinks to the bottom and shellfish do this in the sea. Even shrimp eat carrion, although they also eat plants and smaller animals as well. In addition, mollusks like oysters, clams, mussels, and scallops, filter water, and if the water is contaminated with sewage, these mollusks also become contaminated with sewage. This is how people get viral Hepatitis A infections or bacterial infections like Campylobacter from eating raw or improperly cooked mollusks.

Today large areas of ocean are contaminated with sewage. Farming or harvesting shellfish from these areas is illegal, but harvesting these shellfish illegally is a very lucrative industry and is very common.

Sea water is also becoming increasingly contaminated with heavy metals like mercury, and by filtering the water, mollusks concentrate these heavy metals in their flesh and subsequently pass them on to whatever eats them.

On the other hand, let us look at the health benefits of eating fish that meet God's criteria for healthy food: fish with scales and fins. I believe fish is the healthiest meat we can eat, and was the primary meat that Jesus ate. I am not promoting deep fried fish loaded with grease and high in calories; but grilled, broiled, or baked fish has multiple health benefits. The healthiest fish are the cold water fishes, like salmon, tuna, and sardines. These are the highest in the healthy omega-3 fatty acids (see Chapter 6).

Omega-3 fatty acids from fish oil have been shown to reduce the incidence of mouth, esophagus, stomach, pancreas, colon, and rectal cancers. Those who ate fish just once a week had a 20-30% less risk of these cancers. Those who ate two or more servings of fish per week had a 30-50% less risk of these cancers. This reduction is possibly due to omega-3 fatty acid's ability to inhibit the growth of cancer cells.

Eating fish also reduces the incidence of heart disease. A Harvard School of Public Health study found that in 5,103 women with type 2 diabetes, those that ate fish at least five times a week were 64% less likely to develop heart disease. Furthermore, eating fish just a few times a month reduced the risk of heart disease by 30%.

In another study, the risk of death from heart attack was cut in half by eating an average of eight and a half ounces of fish per week. This benefit in the prevention of heart disease is thought to be due to the benefits of EPA (Eicosapentanoic acid) and DHA (Docosahexanoic acid), the two most prevalent omega-3's found in fish.

The EPA reduces the stickiness of blood platelets which help prevent plaque build up that leads to obstruction of arteries.

The DHA seems to stabilize heart rhythm, especially in patients recovering from myocardial infarction.

In addition, fish with scales and fins contain alkylglycerols that chelates and removes toxic heavy metals like mercury from our bodies.

The next meat source we will look at is fowls. What does God's word saying about this subject? Leviticus 11:13-19 tell us which birds not to eat. What we see again is that we are forbidden to eat scavengers and birds of prey. Presumably, then, we are allowed to eat any bird that does not fall into either of these categories. This fortunately allows us to eat chickens, turkey, quail and most other commonly eaten birds in our culture.

However, whenever eating fish or fowl, the same principles apply to them as applies to other food sources: specifically, the closer the food remains to the state in which it exists in nature the better. This does not mean the meat should be eaten raw—far from it. But it does mean that the meat would be better baked, grilled, or smoked rather than deep fried. When frying food, you add a lot of fat that does not exist in nature, and the extremely high temperatures used in deep frying cause molecular changes (such as the formation of trans-saturated fats), that are not healthy for us.

The other meat source listed in the Bible is insects. The Bible says we can eat locusts, katydids, crickets, and grasshoppers. Before you say "Ugh!" and dismiss everything about the Bible diet, you must realize that although this food source is not incorporated into our culture, it is a common food and protein source for many other cultures. And it almost certainly served as a protein source for the Israelites as they traveled though the wilderness for forty years after their exodus from Egypt. Remember that John the Baptist ate locusts and wild honey as a special form of fast to symbolize his dedication to God's service.

Leviticus 11:29-30 forbids us to eat all reptiles and snakes. These animals frequently carry infections that can be transmitted to humans. Pet turtles were very popular several years ago, but are now banned from being sold to the general public because of several salmonella infection outbreaks that occurred among children playing with them. God said don't eat these animals—so no frog legs!

Now that we have established which meats to eat and not eat, let's talk a little about **quantity**. Although red meat in the form of beef is allowed in God's diet, the amount we eat today is far from the quantity that God intended for us to eat. How do I know? When you read the instruction in God's word on eating beef and sheep, you see that the animal was to be sacrificed first and all the blood and fat was to be burned, then the meat could be eaten. The Israelite nation had seven major feasts a year, and this was when most sacrifices were performed. Thus, the Hebrew nation only ate red meat several times a year.

It has been shown that we can obtain all the nutritional benefit we need from red meat by eating one serving per month. This is not far at all from what the Jewish nation did during the Old Testament times.

The current medical recommendation is to eat red meat no more than three times per week. But it is not unusual for many people to eat red meat three times a day. If you think not, consider that many people will grab a sausage, bacon, ham, or steak biscuit in the morning on their way to work, then a hamburger for lunch, and go home to a pot roast, meatloaf, or steak. Not only do we eat red meat far too frequently, but we are eating excessive amounts.

One serving of red meat is four ounces. That is the size of the patty on a quarter-pounder hamburger. Thus, a 16-ounce T-bone steak is four servings of red meat. So not only do some people eat red meat three times a day, but the total quantity may equal four to six servings a day.

"Do not join those who drink too much wine or gorge themselves on meat, for drunkards and gluttons become poor, and drowsiness clothes them in rags"
Proverbs 23: 20-21.

Excessive protein intake may accelerate osteoporosis by leaching calcium out of your bones, can increase the risk of gouty arthritis, and can be hard on the kidneys. In addition, a high protein-low carbohydrate diet leads to an abnormal metabolic state called ketosis, which if unchecked, can cause many medical problems. Two large studies from Harvard University found a link between colon cancer and red meat intake. **In one of the studies, men who ate red meat five or more times a week have four times the risk of colon cancer compared to those who ate red meat less than once a month.**

"You reap what you eat."

Thus, instead of "upsizing" our meals, we need to downsize them. We should trim as much fat away from red meat as we can before it is cooked. Trimming away the fat after it is cooked is less beneficial because much of the fat is by then absorbed into the meat.

Also, let me clarify another point. Red meat includes composite meats like bologna, hot dogs, potted ham, Spam, and vienna sausages. Plus, many of these contain pork, but even the whole beef products are high in fat and contain left-over parts from the butchering process, including, in some cases, hair.

I personally believe that internal organs such as liver, kidneys, gizzards, and certainly intestines and brains should not be eaten, and Biblical laws confirm this by requiring that these parts be burnt.

Chapter Nine:

Obesitiy and Tips to Lose Weight

"Man eats too much. Thus he lives on only a quarter of what he consumes. The doctors however, live on the remaining three quarters." -an ancient Egyptian doctor, recorded in the Edwin Smith papyrus, approximately 3700 years old

Although this book is a diet book for healthy living, I would be amiss if it did not include a chapter or two on losing weight.

Obesity is becoming an epidemic in America, and unfortunately, the incidence of obesity within the church is no different from the world. If there is a difference, it may be that there is more obesity among church members than among non-churchgoers.

This is unfortunate because this reflects that the church is not doing a good job honoring God by keeping their physical bodies (God's temple) healthy. The real tragedy is that most individuals never think of obesity in this light. We are a society that has almost come to accept obesity as normal. We certainly don't think of obesity as dishonoring God, and we would never purposefully do anything to dishonor our Lord and Savior, but in essence, that is exactly what we are doing if we don't keep God's temple clean and healthy (See Chapter One for further explanation).

As God's children, we are to be a separate people: **"Or what fellowship can light have with darkness? What harmony is there between Christ and Belial? What does a believer have in common with an unbeliever? What agreement is there between the temple of God and idols? For we are the temple of the living God. As God has said: 'I will live with them and walk with them, and I will be their God, and they will be my people.' Therefore come out from them and be separate, says the Lord," 2 Corinthians 6:14b-17a.** We are not to look like or act like non believers. We are to be separate. God lives within us and we are to reflect that in our lives, and in how we treat our bodies. Thus, as God's children, we should endeavor to maintain a healthy weight so the world can see we are honoring God with our bodies.

If you feel you have done everything in your power to lose weight and it hasn't worked, and you have lost hope and the desire to lose weight, the next chapter is for you. But otherwise, I believe the tips in this chapter will benefit you greatly. But like all good ideas, they are useless unless followed and put into practice. This will take willpower and sacrifice, but remember that the sacrifice you make is for your Savior. It is His temple.

One method to lose excess body weight is to eliminate all unnecessary calories. Eliminating just a few calories here and there will mount up over the course of a day.

If you can eliminate 500 calories every day from your normal diet, you will lose one pound a week—that is simply a medical and mathematical fact. If that is true, why is it so hard to lose weight? The answer lies in two key words: "every" and "normal". You must eliminate 500 calories every day to lose one pound a week—in other words, a deficit of 3500 calories (seven days x 500 calories/day) is required to lose one pound. If you only cut out 500 calories two days a week, it will take three and a half weeks to lose one pound. The key, therefore, is consistency—cut out those calories every day. We tend to do well one day and reward ourselves by indulging a little the next day, and of course, by doing so, we lose the benefit of the first day's calorie deficit.

The second key word is "normal". We must eliminate those 500 calories from what we normally eat. It has to be a reduction of 500 calories. Eliminating 500 calories here and adding a few hundred calories somewhere else neutralizes some, if not all of the benefit of the original reduction. Calorie reduction can be quite easy if we are willing to make a few sacrifices.

One excellent way to limit calories is to cut out carbonated soft drinks. Each regular sweetened soft drink beverage contains eight to nine teaspoons of sugar and between 160-200 calories. Cutting out three soft drinks a day will meet the 500-calorie reduction goal and many Americans today could eliminate this many soft drinks daily.

Another easy way to eliminate calories is by cutting out condiments such as butter, margarine, sour cream, salad dressings, gravies, cheese sauces, etc. One tablespoon of margarine or butter contains approximately 100 calories, which can easily be eliminated. I have discovered that without the butter or margarine, you can actually taste the food much better than you could when the same food was covered with the condiment. It only takes about a month to get used to whatever you are eating, so in three to four weeks, you are not even missing the condiment any longer.

The same thing is true with other condiments. Most salad dressings have about seventy-five to 100 calories per tablespoon. Studies have proven you will eat less salad dressing if you get the dressing on the side and dip your lettuce into the dressing rather than pouring the dressing over the lettuce.

If you drink alcoholic beverages, you should stop. Alcohol represents empty calories, because there are few, if any, nutritional benefits from the drink in exchange for the calories you are getting. The best liquids to drink with meals are water, unsweetened tea, and black coffee.

Another obvious way to reduce calorie intake is to reduce the portion size of what you eat. We live in a society where everything encourages us to eat more and more. Restaurants have "all you can eat" salad and food bars, Fast food restaurants encourage us to "upsize" for a few cents more, when in reality, we should pay them to downsize. Serving sizes have increased dramatically in recent decades. Since the mid-1950's, the average carbonated soft drink size has increased from 6.5 ounces to sixteen ounces. A regular order of french fries has increased from 2.4 ounces to seven ounces, and the average portion size of movie theater popcorn has increased from three cups to twenty-one cups. I can remember when a "quarter pound" hamburger was one of the largest on the market, and today it appears quite puny.

When you eat smaller portions, never return for seconds. Eat only until your hunger is satisfied, and don't feel guilty leaving food on your plate—feel wise instead.

Another way to eliminate calories is by choosing how your food is prepared. Food that is baked, grilled, or stir fried will have less calories than the same food fried. Thus, avoid fried chicken, fish, french fries, potato chips, and so forth. These are all high calorie products.

A second method to reduce your excess body weight is to suppress your appetite naturally. One way to do this is by drinking one or two glasses of water prior to your meals (especially your evening meal). A full stomach sends a reflex message to the brain that you are full and should quit eating. The water occupies space and gives you that full sensation sooner.

It has also been shown that the length of time you eat is tied in to this same reflex message of fullness. The longer you eat, the stronger the message to the brain that you are full, regardless of the amount of food eaten. Thus, eat slowly, and you will eat less. This has been proven in several studies. One way to eat slower is to chew your food more thoroughly before swallowing. This also helps the digestive system, since your body is designed for food to be broken into small pieces by chewing and mixing the food particles with saliva, which contain digestive enzymes to start the digestive process. When you eat fast, you bypass this essential step in healthy eating. Conversely, it has also been shown that individuals who eat fast eat more food before they feel full.

Another way to naturally suppress your appetite is to eat high protein foods like nuts, seeds, or peanut butter about thirty minutes prior to your meal. High protein foods give you a full feeling. A small handful of nuts or sunflower seeds, or a tablespoon of peanut butter is all it takes to suppress your appetite enough to eat less during the subsequent meal. I use this trick frequently. In the evenings when I get home from work, my wife has dinner ready. I eat a small handful of mixed nuts at my office a few minutes before I leave to go home. By the time I sit down to eat supper I feel less hungry.

Moderate exercise thirty to sixty minutes prior to a meal is another way to naturally suppress the appetite.

A third method to lose excess weight is to distribute your caloric intake differently. The average American today consumes his largest meal of the day at dinner, when he least needs the calories for energy. Furthermore, dinner time is getting later and later, so many people now eat dinner just one or two hours prior to bedtime.

In fact, the largest meal of the day should ideally be breakfast, but that, in reality, is very difficult for most of us to achieve. However, you should never skip breakfast. In fact, you should not skip any meals. Eating three small meals a day is better than eating one or two big meals a day, especially if you want to lose weight. Distributing the calories throughout the day gives you a better opportunity to use those calories for energy rather than storing them as fat. You should ideally strive to eat two-thirds of the day's total calories by mid-afternoon, and never eat dinner later than two hours prior to bedtime.

A fourth method to lose weight is, of course, to burn more calories. This involves regular aerobic exercise. Calories are burned while you are exercising. The number of calories expended depends upon the type of exercise, the duration of the time spent exercising, the intensity at which the exercise is performed, your body size, and other factors. The benefits of exercise, however, is not limited to the number of calories utilized while performing the exercise. The real benefit of exercise is that exercise increases your metabolism, so you burn more calories even while sleeping. How does exercise increase metabolism? First, exercise increases muscle mass and muscles utilize calories more effectively than other tissues. Second, aerobic exercise increases a cellular structure called oxidative mitochondria, which is the "power house of the cell", and the more oxidative mitochondria you have, the higher your metabolism. You should strive to exercise at least twenty to thirty minutes daily. Please note that work does not constitute exercise. You may indeed walk two miles a day at work or climb steps repeatedly, but work is stop/go activity, and does not increase oxidative mitochondria or have as much cardiovascular benefits as true exercise. True exercise is sustained activity (non-stop) performed at a fast enough pace to reach a target heart rate [approximately 85% of (220 minus your age)] for at least fifteen to twenty minutes.

For example, exercise could be a sustained, non-stop, brisk walk performed at a fast enough pace to be a little out of breath, but still able to talk to someone walking with you.

Another simple way to burn more calories is to lower your thermostat in the winter, especially at night while you sleep. The lower the environmental temperature, the more calories your body has to burn to maintain body temperature. Lowering your thermostat just a few degrees can help.

The fifth method to help you lost weight is to eat only foods on the Bible diet. For example, eat only whole grain products and no refined flour products. Avoid refined table sugar as much as possible. Avoid saturated fat from red meat and dairy products. Eat only lean red meat in moderation, and fat free or low fat dairy products. Avoid trans saturated products like cookies, crackers, margarines, french fries, potato chips, donuts, etc. This dietary information is given in much more detail in other sections of this book.

Losing weight is possible, and it is not even that difficult, it just requires consistency, dedication, and some sacrifice.

As you lose weight, you will feel better, gain more energy, have a better self-image, and have a knowledge that you are honoring God by helping to make your body healthier.

If you have been obese for a long time and you feel that there is no way that these or any other suggestions will work for you, then perhaps you need to read the next chapter. The next chapter was not planned, it was given to me as a dream. I dreamed one Saturday morning that I was in my office and a very obese lady was sitting on the exam table. She was very discouraged about her weight, and was sharing with me many of the thoughts and feelings expressed in the next chapter. I felt helpless to do anything for her and prayed for God to give me the wisdom to know what to tell her. The Holy Spirit then began to give me scriptures to share with this lady. When I awoke from my dream, I shared my experience with my wife and then recorded everything I remembered. The results are Chapter Ten. I cannot take credit for this chapter, I believe it was revealed to me by God.

Chapter Ten:

The Defeated Overweight Individual

Let me see if I can describe you: you can hardly remember when you were not overweight. You have tried every diet imaginable. Some of these diets you actually lost weight on, but as soon as you came off the diet you gained the weight back. Besides, food is your best friend. It is your reward. When you feel depressed, lonely, bored, angry, jealous, or afraid, food gives you comfort and pleasure that you get nowhere else. Your friends are only superficial at best and aren't really there to support you when you need them the most. Your spouse now only looks at you with contempt in his/her eyes, because they are disgusted at your weight and physical appearance. Your spouse is mad at you, thinks you are weak or lazy and have no self-control. Perhaps your spouse even thinks that you are being passively aggressive and got fat just to let him/her know you are not happy in your relationship. Your spouse has distanced himself/herself from you and is no longer intimate. You think it is too late now to lose weight—the damage is already done. Your relationship with those you loved and with those who loved you has already been damaged beyond repair. You have damaged your body, and health problems are now developing or are already well established. You can't quit eating, nor do you want to; eating is the only pleasure left in your life, it is your only friend. You are mad at God for giving you this lot in life, for giving you this body and this weakness that you cannot overcome. If this describes you, then you are the "defeated overweight person," and if you are a Christian, then you are the "defeated overweight Christian". If this describes your thoughts and feelings, then Satan has you exactly where he wants you to be, and that is "defeated". You are of very little use to the kingdom of God when you are defeated. Your damaged relationship with your family, your low self esteem, your damaged health, and the resultant damage to God's temple (your body) all thrill Satan, and he is very happy as long as you stay defeated.

You may now be thinking that all is hopeless. I have damaged myself and my relationship with family and friends beyond repair. I cannot stay on a diet for two months, much less the rest of my life. I have no willpower, and now I have the forces of Satan against me. All is hopeless.

I have good news for you: it is not hopeless. The future has never been brighter for you. I can share with you the solution to your problem, and can tell you about the relationship that can never be severed.

The Defeated Overweight Individual

If you are a born again Christian (not just a church member), you are a child of the King, a child of the sovereign God (El Shaddai), the God of healing (Jehovah Rapha), and of the God who provides (Jehovah Jireh). Your Father provides everything you need to overcome defeat and to be a champion. If you are not a Christian and do not know this God we are referring to, turn to Appendix A now and discover how to become a child of the King.

How does being a child of God help you overcome defeat? Well, let's look at what the Bible says.

First of all, the relationship with you and your heavenly Father can never be destroyed: **"For I am convinced that neither death nor life, neither angels nor demons, neither the present nor the future, nor any powers, neither height nor depth, nor anything else in all creation, will be able to separate us from the love of God that is in Christ Jesus our Lord" (Romans 8:38-39).** God will love you unconditionally, despite your shortcomings and your physical appearance. He loved you enough to send His only son to die for you (see Appendix A), and when you accept His son, Jesus Christ, as your Lord and Savior, then you are His for all eternity. **"And do not grieve the Holy Spirit of God with whom you were sealed for the day of redemption," Ephesians 4:30.** When we are born again, we receive the Holy Spirit, with which we are sealed for all eternity. Even if you have been unfaithful, even if you have been angry with God, He will still be faithful to you: **"If we are faithless, he will remain faithful, for he cannot disown himself" (2 Timothy 2:13).** You see, it is not just your life and body that we are dealing with here. When you gave your life to Jesus and his Holy Spirit sealed you for the day of redemption, you became His. He is living through you. Your body is His temple. **"For we who are alive are always being given over to death for Jesus's sake, so that his life may be revealed in our mortal body," 2 Corinthians 4:11. "Do you not know your body is a temple of the Holy Spirit, who is in you, whom you have received from God? You are not your own, you were bought at a price. Therefore, honor God with your body," 1 Corinthians 6:19.** Now, if Jesus has a personal love for you that is unconditional (and He does), and if Jesus has a personal interest in your body (and He does), then you can trust that Jesus will help you overcome any weakness you may have that keeps you from honoring Him with your body.

What kind of help is available for you as a child of the King? **"Therefore you do not lack any spiritual gift as you eagerly wait for our Lord Jesus Christ to be revealed. He will keep you strong to the end, so that you will be blameless on the day of our Lord Jesus Christ," 1 Corinthians 1:7-8.** You have every spiritual gift you need to accomplish God's will in your life. You have every resource that Jesus had—hard to imagine, but true. We are sons and daughters of the Almighty God (El Shaddai), and we have every resource that he can provide. There is more than enough to set you free from any bondage you are facing. You do not have to be mastered by food. **"Everything is permissible for me"—but not everything is beneficial. "Everything is permissible for me"—but I will not be mastered by anything, (1 Corinthians 6:12).** You do not have to be burdened by anxiety: **"Cast your cares on the Lord and he will sustain you; he will never let the righteous fall," (Psalm 55:22)**. If you are committed to doing His will in your life, He will never let you fall. You do not need to live your life in fear of failure: **"I sought the Lord and he answered me, he delivered me from all my fears," (Psalm 34:4)**. Your lack of self discipline is not a problem because God's spirit that lives in you has plenty. **"For God did not give us a spirit of timidity, but a spirit of power, of love and of self discipline."** And even Satan cannot keep you from becoming what God wants you to become. **"Submit yourselves, then, to God. Resist the devil, and he will flee from you. Come near to God and he will come near to you," (James 4:7-8)**.

Submit your life now to God, our Heavenly Father, the God who provides for our every need (Jehovah Jireh), and He will do the rest. If you truly let Him be your Lord as well as your Savior, He will set you free from every bondage in your life. You have never been truly free until Jesus sets you free. **"So if the Son sets you free, you will be free indeed," (John 8:36)**.

God will take away your cravings for foods you do not need. God will take away your fears and anxieties that you currently treat by eating to satisfy the flesh. When you realize that you are a child of the God that created the entire universe and that you have every benefit that comes from being His son or daughter, it is difficult to have a low self-esteem. God can and will help you overcome your obesity, but you must submit to Him. You need to study His word, you must pray to Him daily, especially when you are tempted to eat unneccessarily.

You must eat only the foods that He gave us to enjoy, be thankful for them, and ask Him to bless these foods to your health. You have failed before because you used your strength. But you must use God's strength instead, **"I can do everything through him who gives me strength," (Phillipians 4:13).** When you truly submit your life to Jesus Christ and make him Lord of your life, then he will begin living through you and your obesity will be no match to the one who has power and authority over all things. **"Then Jesus came to them and said, 'All authority in heaven and on earth has been given to me,'" (Matthew 28:18).**

Chapter Eleven:

Fasting

"Instead of using medicine, fast a day"
-Plutarch (46-120 AD)

Any book written about biblical dietary guidelines must contain something about fasting to be complete. Fasting is an essential component of God's plan pertaining to our consumption of food. The benefits of fasting have been observed throughout history (as indicated by Plutarch's quote at the start of the chapter), but the Bible makes it very clear that Christians are to fast for spiritual purposes. The health benefits are an added bonus, but do exist. Isaiah 58:8 refers to the healing power of fasting.

Many modern day Christians have the same attitude toward fasting as they do toward God's dietary restrictions: specifically, that those rules don't apply to us today. The problem is, God's word says otherwise.

In the Sermon on the Mount, Jesus is instructing New Testament believers. He teaches them to give to the needy and to pray and to fast. Jesus never says, "If you fast", he says, "When you fast". The inference is that we will fast.

In addition, in **Matthew 9:15** Jesus is being asked by John's disciples why His disciples did not fast. Jesus responded, **"How can the guests of the bridegroom mourn while he is with them? The time will come when the bridegroom will be taken from them; then they will fast"** (emphasis mine). The bridegroom was taken from us when Jesus died on the cross, and was ressurected and ascended to the right hand of God the Father. Now is the time that Jesus said his disciples would fast.

Multiple other passages throughout the Old and New Testaments make it clear that fasting is as essential as prayer to keep a right relationship with our Lord and Savior. But what does fasting have to do with the Bible diet?

First of all, fasting requires discipline, just as following God's dietary laws requires discipline. In both, we are saying to God that honoring Him is more important than satisfying our flesh. We are saying, "I am willing to make a personal sacrifice of pleasure and comfort to worship you, God. (and to get) closer to you. (In essense), God is more important than food." God honors men and women who fervently seek Him. **Romans 12:11** says, **"Never be lacking in zeal, but keep your spiritual fervor, serving the Lord." James 5:16** states, **"The effectual fervent prayer of a righteous man availeth much"** (King James Version). When we fast, we are essentially dying to ourselves and our desires in order to become more aware of God's desire in our lives.

There are many good books written on fasting, and I encourage you to get one, read it, and pray about what God would have you do in your life.

There are definite medical benefits to be obtained from fasting. One of the benefits of fasting seems to be the removal of toxins stored in fat tissue. A prolonged fast, especially, forces the body to break down fat for energy, thus releasing stored toxins.

Some studies have shown dramatic improvement in asthmatics and allergy sufferers after a fast. Fasting has also been implicated as beneficial for patients suffering from arthritis, [1]psoriasis, and irritable bowel syndrome.

Fasting has been shown to have favorable effects on the bacterial flora of the intestines, lowering blood pressure and an overall improvement in a variety of medical conditions.

Colin Campbell, PhD, professor of Nutritional Biochemistry at Cornell University, has shown that fasting effectively lowers high blood pressure.

In a country where the general population are gluttons, the concept of fasting is not a popular one, but perhaps we would be wise to listen to what God said about the sin of Sodom and Gomorrah. Everyone thinks that their sin was sodomy or homosexuality, but the Bible teaches that this was just a symptom of their disease. Their true sin is recorded in Ezekiel 16:49-50, **"Now this was the sin of your sister Sodom: she and her daughters were arrogant, overfed, and unconcerned; they did not help the poor and needy. They were haughty and did detestable things before me. Therefore I did away with them as you have seen."** Sodom had become prosperous, arrogant, and overfed. And they forgot the Lord. Sound familiar? Our country has become complacent, arrogant, overfed, and is merciless. I pray that we change before God has to judge us as He judged Sodom.

Endnotes

[1] *psoriasis* - a chronic skin condition

Chapter Twelve:
Choices

Why is there a Bible diet? Why did God spend time giving detailed information to ancient patriarchs like Moses, Noah, and Adam concerning what to eat and not to eat? Why do foods that are healthy for you taste like broccoli and foods that are bad for you taste like ice cream?

Basically, I believe it all comes down to spiritual issues. Throughout life, from the time we reach the age of accountability until we die, our lives consist of a series of choices. God made us to be creatures of free choice, beginning with Adam and Eve. He wants us to choose to love Him and to choose to worship Him. He also wants us to choose to obey Him and to choose to have faith in Him.

Thus, when we get right down to it, our dietary choices really reflect our willingness to obey God and faith that what He says is true; or our decision of satisfying self, pleasing our own flesh and believing that we know what is best for our well being. Basically, making ourselves a god.

This is the same scenario we see with the very first man and woman. God placed Adam and Eve in the Garden of Eden and gave them "all kinds of trees growing out of the ground—trees that were pleasing to the eye and good for food," (Genesis 1:9). He only forbade them to eat from one tree—but He gave them free choice to obey Him or not. Satan tempted Eve, and said something like this: "Go ahead and eat the forbidden food; it won't harm you, but if you eat it your eyes will be opened to real truth and you will be a god."

Satan still uses those same temptations today. The issue is the same. Will you believe God's word, trust Him and obey Him, believing His plan is best for your health and life?

God could have made every food as good for you as broccoli yet taste as good as ice cream, but He chose not to. So, we have to make a choice. Will you eat what God says is good for you, even if you don't like the taste; and will you refuse the forbidden foods, even if you enjoy them? It is a matter of personal sacrifice. Just like fasting, it is a matter of denying what pleases you to do instead what pleases God. **Hebrews 11:6 says, "And without faith it is impossible to please God, because anyone who comes to him must believe that he exists and that he rewards those who earnestly seek him."**

Satan wants to see our bodies weak, polluted, and riddled by disease. In such a condition, our ability to work for God is severely compromised and God's temple (our bodies) is defiled. What could make Satan happier?

When we say we are "tempted" to eat a food that we know is not in our best interest, we don't consider how accurate that statement really is. It is a temptation of Satan and of the flesh to eat unhealthy foods.

But take heart. If you are born again and have placed your faith in the Lord Jesus Christ, you have everything within you that is needed to overcome such temptation. (If you do not know Jesus Christ as your Lord and Savior, but are interested, please see now how to come to know him by following the steps in Appendix A.) If you are born again, you have the Holy Spirit living within you. The Bible teaches us the **"fruit of the Spirit is love, joy, peace, patience, kindness, goodness, faithfulness, gentleness, and self-control," (Galatians 5:22).**

You see, the fruit of the Holy Spirit gives you self-control. You can overcome temptations of the flesh and temptations of the world and of Satan, if you ask for and accept God's help. **"I can do all things through Him who strengthens me," (Phillipians 4:13).**

God is interested in every aspect of your life, not just the spiritual. He is interested in the emotional, social, intellectual, and physical aspects of your life. He desires to lead and guide you in every aspect. The Bible says that if we are saved, the Holy Spirit is our life. We should live like it. **"Since we live by the spirit, let us keep in step with the spirit," (Galatians 5:25).** Let the Holy Spirit lead you in your interpretation of this book and in your choices to live a healthy life for the glory of God!

Appendix A:
The ABC's of Salvation

1. Admit that you have sinned and are a sinner. **"For all have sinned and come short of the glory of God"**
Romans 3:23.
Sinners cannot enter heaven. Sin must be punished. The punishment of sin is death. But God loved us so much he provided the death sacrifice for our sins. **"For God so loved the world, that he gave his only begotten son, that whosoever believeth in him should not perish, but have everlasting life,"**
John 3:16 (King James Version)
Jesus came to earth, lived a perfect sinless life and then gave His life to die on the cross to pay the penalty for you and me.

2. Believe in the Lord Jesus Christ.
   Believe He is God's son, that He died on the cross for your sins, and that His death was sufficient to pay the penalty for your sins. There is no other way. **"I am the way, the truth, and the life: no man cometh unto the Father, but by me,"**
   (John 14:6, KJV).
   "But as many as received him, to them gave he power to become the sons of God, even to them that believe on his name,"
   (John 1:12, KJV).
   We are saved (born again) when we give our life to Jesus. We are saved by faith. Faith that Jesus is Lord and is capable of meeting all our needs. Faith is not just believing facts about Jesus, but by trusting every aspect of your life to Him. We must put Him before everything and everyone and turn from our old sinful life.

3. Confess with our mouths and with our lives that Jesus is our Lord. **"That if thou shalt confess with thy mouth the Lord Jesus, and shalt believe in thine heart that God hath raised him from the dead, thou shalt be saved,"**
   (Romans 10:9, KJV).
   Jesus did not remain dead. After He died on the cross, He was buried, and on the third day He was resurrected (came back to life), and now sits in heaven at the right hand of God the Father to intercede on our behalf. He is waiting to hear you pray right now. He wants to hear you pray the

sinner's prayer. It goes something like this, but you need to pray from your heart.

God, I am a sinner and I know that unless my sins are forgiven I will go to Hell. I believe you sent your son, Jesus Christ, to die on the cross to pay the penalty for my sins. I believe you raised Him from the dead and He now lives. I accept the gift of Jesus's death, and I now give my life to Him so that He may live through me. I will make Jesus the Lord of my life. Thank you, God, for forgiving and washing away my sins. Thank you for making me a new person. I love you.

                            Amen.

If you pray the prayer sincerely from your heart and believe it, then you will be born again and you will become a new creature. **"Therefore, if any man be in Christ, he is a new creature: old things are passed away; behold, all things are become new,"**
                    (2 Corinthians 5:17, KJV).

Appendix B:

Personal Testimony

I know that by this time the average reader is going to be thinking "This Rick Mays guy has got to be some kind of religious zealot or Jesus freak, and I believe he has gone off the deep end". Well, the truth is, I am a Jesus freak, if that is what you want to call someone who places God first in their life. The other fact is that there was probably no person more unlikely to write this book than myself. Let me explain what I mean by sharing my personal testimony with you so you can see how God's plans are not always our plans.

I was "born again" as a young child at Vacation Bible School. I was fully aware at that young age that I was a sinner and needed forgiveness of those sins, and believed with all my heart that if I gave my life to Jesus Christ that my sins would be forgiven; and they were.

At the age of twelve I felt called to become a doctor, and shared that dream with my parents. From that moment on, I never doubted that I would one day become a physician and never changed my mind about my desire. My dream became a reality only because God opened door after door and made it possible for me to fulfill my calling. However, this only became obvious to me much later in my life; I did not realize it at the time.

During those years I was very opinionated about many things. One thing was that since I had dedicated my life to science, I had no need for the arts or literature. I despised English classes and only took the minimal requirements in both high school and college. A college professor even tried to talk me into taking another class with the warning that, "One day, you might be a physician and decide to write a book". I found that suggestion very humorous and unfortunately, did not take the class.

Another thing I was sure of was that I did not want to be a family physician. I wanted to be an orthopedic surgeon. I was in my third year of medical school before I changed my mind and went into family medicine. The change of mind occurred because after doing two months of orthopedics in my clinical years of medical school, I was extremely bored. My advisor suggested that if I wanted variety I should go into family medicine. Reluctantly I tried it, fell in love with it, and have been well satisfied with my chosen specialty ever since.

In addition, I was bored to tears with every lecture in medical school that dealt with nutrition. I was convinced that nutrition was basic common sense. Everyone knew what to eat and I had more important things to be concerned over.

Being raised in the country in southeastern Kentucky, I grew up eating wild game including squirrel, rabbit, frog legs, snapping turtle, and plenty of pork. As I grew older my palate expanded to include all kinds of shell fish, and I dearly loved shrimp, oysters, crab legs, scallops, and lobster.

So you see, here I am, a person who never had much experience with writing or basic English skills and no experience with public speaking, with very little use for nutrition, who loved to eat pretty much anything that was not still moving, writing this book. The concept seemed unlikely and impractical to me and so it took a while to convince myself that I should do this.

Eventually, I convinced myself to try, but after a few years I got confused. I started out writing this book for the general population with very few spiritual references. Then I started making it more of a scientific exposition on diet and its effect on the human body. Finally, through a series of events, God convinced me He wanted this book written for His children, for those that truly believed in His sovereignty. Once I had reached a decision concerning the audience God wanted the book to reach, writing it became much easier—for a while. Then about a year ago, I reached a stalemate. It seemed that no matter how hard I tried, I couldn't finish the book. I prayed about it and God showed me that I could not finish this book because I had not changed my life and diet to be obedient to the statutes God had revealed to me and recorded in His holy word. I was convinced that God still wants His people to follow His dietary laws, yet I had not been willing to give up the foods I loved so dearly.

The second week of February 2004 I was driving to the hospital to make rounds and I clearly heard God speak two simple words to me, "It's time". I immediately knew in my heart what he meant. God told me that it was time to become obedient and submit to His dietary laws and to finish this book. I came home and talked to my wife about my desire to follow the Bible diet and she agreed to help and support me. Since that time, I have been as compliant as possible in following God's dietary laws and I have, in addition to finishing this book, seen many changes take place in my health. I want to share with you some of the changes that I have experienced in my personal health as a result of following God's plan.

When I started the Bible diet in mid-February, I weighed 222 pounds, which at 6'2", was overweight. Not quite six months later, as I am finishing this book, I weigh 204 pounds. My waist circumference has decreased from 41 3/4 inches to 37 inches in the same period of time. This was accomplished without much effort on my part, except for compliance to the Bible diet. I did not reduce the quantitiy of food I ate. I skipped no meals and never went hungry. But I ate no foods restricted in the Bible diet, such as pork and shellfish. I also made sure that almost all flour products I ate were 100% whole grain and I eliminated most red meat from my diet. I eat red meat about once or twice a month.

Medically, there were some improvements in my health as well. My energy level improved. I was having lots of joint and muscle aches and pains that have improved. My blood pressure went from 134/86 on February 23, to 128/92 on March 8, to 128/80 on June 15; and the diastolic (lower) reading has remained 80 or less since June. A normal blood pressure reading is 140/85 or less, depending on other medical conditions you may have.

The most exciting change, however, was my cholesterol. I had always been convinced that I had an inherited form of high cholesterol. Many of the males in my family have high cholesterol and/or triglycerides. Mine has been high since the first time I was checked as a young man. I tried the American Heart Association (AHA) diet, and it had no effect on my cholesterol numbers. I then added medication—first starting on Niacin, a B vitamin that has been shown to lower cholesterol and triglycerides, but it had little benefit. I then added a statin type medication (this is the most common type of medication prescribed to lower cholesterol—medicines like Zocor, Lipitor, Pravachol, Lescol, etc.), and increased it to the highest recommended dosage. Thus, on a maximal dose of a statin medication along with Niacin and the AHA diet, my total cholesterol was 273, the bad LDL cholesterol was 193, triglycerides were 239, and the good HDL cholesterol was 32.

When I started the Bible diet in February, I stopped all medications. By June 14, 2004, my total cholesterol had come down to 208, the bad (LDL) cholesterol was down to 146, triglycerides were 121, and the good (HDL) cholesterol had improved to 38. This was without any medication. I never thought I would be able to have normal cholesterol levels, much less to have normal levels without taking medication. Although my cholesterol numbers are still not normal, I truly believe they will be with more time, as long as I stay obedient to God's dietary plan.

I hope you have a similar experience to mine as you experience the power of God released when you are obedient to His will.

About The Author

Richard H. Mays M. D. has a Bachelor of Science degree from Cumberland College in Williamsburg, Kentucky with a double major in Mathematics and Chemistry. He received his medical degree from the University of Kentucky Medical School and completed a three year residency program in Family Medicine at the University of Tennessee in Knoxville.

Dr. Mays is board certified with the American Board of Family Physicians and has been in private practice since 1987.

He now resides in Knoxville, TN. with his wife and three daughters. He enjoys playing basketball, hiking and is an avid gardener.

Printed in Great Britain
by Amazon